FOCUS ON ABILITY

Serving Girls with Special Needs

Girl Scouts of the U.S.A.
420 Fifth Avenue
New York, N.Y. 10018-2798

 GIRL SCOUTS OF THE U.S.A.®

Elinor Johnstone Ferdon, *National President*
Marsha Johnson Evans, *National Executive Director*

Inquiries related to *Focus on Ability: Serving Girls with Special Needs* should be directed to Membership and Program, Girl Scouts of the U.S.A., 420 Fifth Avenue, New York, N.Y. 10018-2798.

Authors
Martha E. Carroll, Ed.D., University of Toledo,
    national operational volunteer, Girl Scouts of the U.S.A.
Martha Jo Dennison, Ed.D.

Contributors
Candace White Ciraco, Ed.D.
Sharon Woods Hussey
Sue Thornton

Editor
Susan Eno

Illustrator
C. A. Trachok

Design and Page Make-up
Keithley and Associates, Inc.

This book may not be reproduced in whole or in part in any form or by any means, electronic or mechanical, including photocopying, recording, or by any information storage and retrieval system now known or hereafter invented, without the prior written permission of Girl Scouts of the United States of America, 420 Fifth Avenue, New York, N.Y. 10018-2798.

Pages 10–11 ("Analysis of a Site"), page 20 ("Math Exercise"), pages 25–27 ("The Lion" and "Alice"), and pages 95–98 ("Overview of ADA, IDEA, and Section 504") may be reproduced by Girl Scout councils without obtaining permission from Girl Scouts of the U.S.A.

© 1998 by Girl Scouts of the United States of America
All rights reserved
First Impression 1998
Printed in the United States of America

ISBN 0-88441-492-2

10 9 8 7 6 5 4 3 2

Contents

Chapter 1 **Introduction**   *1*
    Diversity in Girl Scouting   *2*
    Differences Are on a Continuum   *2*
    Legal Definitions of Disabilities   *3*
    Inclusion in Girl Scouting   *4*

Chapter 2 **Preparing Your Troop or Group**   *6*
    1. Preparing Yourself   *6*
    2. Preparing the Girls   *8*
    3. Preparing the Meeting Environment   *9*
    4. Introducing the Girl to the Troop or Group   *9*
    5. Preparing the Activities   *12*

Chapter 3 **Simulating Disabilities**   *16*
    1. Taking a Spelling Test   *17*
    2. Writing Sentences   *18*
    3. Writing on Paper on Your Forehead   *18*
    4. Writing and Swinging Your Foot   *18*
    5. Writing with Pliers   *19*
    6. Taking a Math Test   *19*
    7. Placing Cotton in Your Ears   *21*
    8. Wearing Distorted Glasses   *21*
    9. Wearing a Blindfold   *22*
    10. Using Mirror Writing   *22*
    11. Using Wheelchairs, Canes, and Crutches   *23*
    12. Reading Paragraphs   *24*
    13. Public Speaking   *28*
    14. Buttoning a Shirt   *28*
    15. Threading a Needle   *29*
    Conclusion   *29*

Chapter 4 **Learning Disabilities**   *30*
    Myths and Stereotypes   *31*
    Characteristics   *32*
    Adaptations for Girls with Learning Disabilities   *34*
    Famous People   *37*

Chapter 5 Communication Disorders — *38*
    Classifications *39*
    Myths and Stereotypes *39*
    Characteristics *39*
    Adaptations for Girls with Communication Disorders *40*
    Famous People *42*

Chapter 6 Mental Retardation — *43*
    A Definition of Mental Retardation *43*
    The Inclusion of Girls with Mental Retardation in Girl Scouting *44*
    Myths and Stereotypes *44*
    Characteristics *45*
    Adaptations for Girls Who Have Mental Retardation *47*
    Famous People *51*

Chapter 7 Behavior Disorders — *52*
    Myths and Stereotypes *53*
    Characteristics *54*
    Adaptations for Girls with Behavior Disorders *55*
    Famous People *59*

Chapter 8 Hearing Impairments — *60*
    Factors to Consider in Adapting Activities *60*
    Myths and Stereotypes *61*
    Characteristics *62*
    Adaptations for Girls with Hearing Impairments *64*
    Famous People *67*

Chapter 9 Visual Impairments — *68*
    Classifications *68*
    Myths and Stereotypes *70*
    Characteristics *70*
    Adaptations for Girls with Visual Impairments *74*
    Famous People *77*

Chapter 10 Physical Disabilities and Health Impairments — *78*
    Physical Disabilities *78*
    Health Impairments *85*
    Myths and Stereotypes *92*
    Famous People *93*

Appendix: Overview of ADA, IDEA, and Section 504 — 95

Resource Information — 99

References — 106

Index — 107

Chapter 1

Introduction

The purpose of this book is to introduce adults in Girl Scouting to the rewards, pleasures, and challenges of working with girls who have disabilities. Girl Scouting is for all girls, and in order for girls with disabilities to be provided with the opportunity to reach their full potential, any barriers that prevent them from participating in the mainstream of Girl Scouting must be removed. Included in this book are definitions of various disabling conditions, ways in which activities can be adapted, and behavioral expectations. Also included are some activities for simulation of the disabling conditions. These simulation activities help to create an awareness of the barriers that people with disabilities experience in society.

Disabilities are more common than is generally believed. Approximately 12 percent of school-age individuals have a disabling condition that inhibits general functioning and requires special assistance or aids in order for the person to participate fully in society (U.S. Department of Education, 1996). By provid-

ing the needed support, the Girl Scout troop or group can include all girls no matter the diversity of their abilities. This does not necessarily require training in special education or therapeutic recreation, but rather a willingness to get to know each girl, an interest in facilitating interaction, and a belief in the benefits of inclusion for everyone.

DIVERSITY IN GIRL SCOUTING

Within each troop or group is a world of diversity and a wide variety of talents and abilities. Some girls can run fast and some cannot. Some do well on tasks that require a great deal of fine detail, such as sewing and drawing; others cannot do these tasks well. Some girls are outgoing and others are ill at ease with children their own age. All of the differences within the troop or group add to the excitement and rewards of being a leader. The challenge is to blend the differences together into a working group or troop, and yet allow each girl to remain an individual with her unique strengths and weaknesses.

DIFFERENCES ARE ON A CONTINUUM

As the leader, you may have noticed that each girl in your troop or group functions according to her individual ability in a particular area. These ranges of ability form continuums and apply for girls with disabilities as well as girls without disabilities. Each girl's level of skill will be located at a certain point on each continuum. Five major continuums are important to the Girl Scout leader:

1. *Learning:* the ability to understand new ideas and to master new skills.
2. *Communication:* the ability to read, understand, and convey ideas through speaking and writing.
3. *Motor and physical ability:* the ability to move about, use tools, and manipulate objects.

4. *Emotional adjustment:* the ability to accept personal strengths and weaknesses and to react to situations in a socially appropriate manner.
5. *Sensory abilities:* the capacity to hear, feel, see, smell, and taste.

Girls who have difficulty using their hands are placed at the low end of the continuum on sewing or writing. However, these same girls may be able to speak in public very well and could be placed at the high end of the continuum when public speaking is the skill being considered.

Some examples of continuums are:

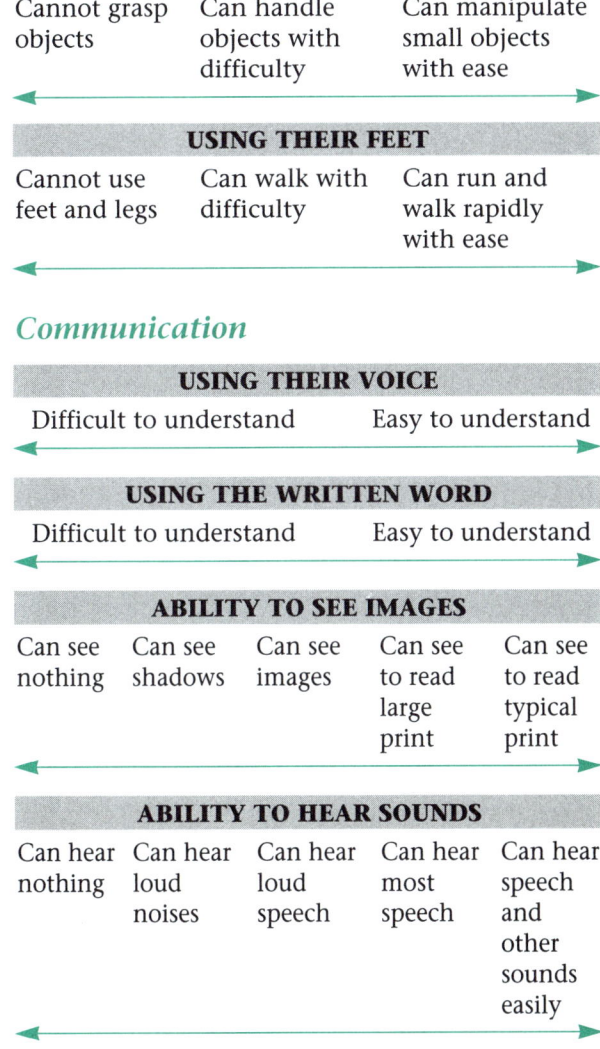

The girl with a disability is not different in an overall sense. She is placed at a different location on a *particular* continuum. It is a mistake to think that the disability will affect all continuums.

A sensitive Girl Scout leader will see each girl as having a combination of high and low skill levels, and must shape activities so that all girls, regardless of their positions on the continuums, may participate. All Girl Scouts, both with and without disabilities, challenge the leader's ability to be creative, sensitive, and energetic.

LEGAL DEFINITIONS OF DISABILITIES

Following are the legal definitions used to determine eligibility for special education and other services for people with disabilities. They are also used by the judicial system in court cases.

According to the Americans with Disabilities Act (ADA) of 1990, a person with a disability is defined as one who meets at least one of the following criteria:

1. Is substantially impaired with respect to a major life activity.
2. Has a record of such an impairment.
3. Is regarded as having such an impairment.

The law does not define particular disabilities. The ADA ensures the same basic civil rights for people with disabilities that nondisabled people already take for granted in housing, transportation, communications, and public access to buildings and activities, including those in Girl Scouting.

The legal definition for each category of disability can be found in the Individuals with Disabilities Education Act (IDEA) of 1990. A girl with a disability will have any of the following: specific learning disabilities, speech or language impairments, mental retardation, serious emotional disturbance, multiple disabilities, hearing impairments, orthopedic impairments, other health impairments, visual impairments, autism, deaf-blindness, and traumatic brain injury. In addition, Section 504 of the Rehabilitation Act of 1973 provides protection for students who may have a disability but do not qualify for special education services.

In the chapters that follow, you will notice some of the categories from IDEA as chapter headings, while others are included within other chapters. Some states may use different terms in legal documents, and may have even more stringent guidelines than federal laws. You should be familiar with the particular legal terms used in your state. For ease and consistency, the federal terms are used here and elsewhere in this book. For a comparison of the ADA, IDEA, and Section 504 facts, see the Appendix.

INCLUSION IN GIRL SCOUTING

Approximately 95 percent of school-age children with disabilities are in regular school settings. Most are integrated into regular classrooms for part or all of the school day (U.S. Department of Education, 1996). Two terms generally associated with schools, and applied to Girl Scouting, are mainstreaming and inclusion. While both mean the integration of Girl Scouts with disabilities into a troop or group predominantly made up of nondisabled Girl Scouts, the term inclusion more closely follows the purpose of Girl Scouting. Inclusion means that all girls plan and participate in all activities. Adaptations are made when needed so that everyone can take part.

As educational and social services move toward more inclusive programs, traditional categories are giving way to analyses of individual needs so that appropriate supports can

be provided. Among schoolchildren who have disabilities, the majority have disabilities that are not physical (see table). Therefore, for most Girl Scouts with disabilities, removing architectural barriers alone will not make Girl Scouting accessible. For that reason, use this book in its entirety, rather than focusing exclusively on a specific chapter. Some of the suggestions in a particular chapter may be appropriate for use with girls with other characteristics. For example, the chapter on communication disorders is useful not only when working with girls with speech and language disorders, but also when working with individuals who have learning disabilities, have cerebral palsy, or speak English as a second language, among others. Likewise, the chapter on behavior disorders can help in providing behavioral strategies for girls who have emotional disturbances, attention deficit disorders, hearing impairments, or even no disability at all. Try looking at each girl's abilities, and the supports needed for inclusion, rather than at a particular label or disability. Inclusion then becomes a more natural process.

PERCENTAGE OF SCHOOL-AGE POPULATION IDENTIFIED BY PRIMARY DISABILITY

Disability	Total Numbers	Percent of Total Ages 6–21
Specific learning disabilities	2,513,977	51.1
Speech or language impairments	1,023,665	20.8
Mental retardation	570,855	11.6
Serious emotional disturbance	428,168	8.7
Other health impairments	106,509	2.2
Multiple disabilities	89,646	1.8
Hearing impairments	65,568	1.3
Orthopedic impairments	60,604	1.2
Visual impairments	24,877	0.5
Autism	22,780	0.5
Traumatic brain injury	7,188	0.2
Deaf-blindness	1,331	0.1
All disabilities	4,915,168	100.0

Source: Adapted from U.S. Department of Education, Office of Special Education Programs, Data Analysis System (DANS).
Note: For 1994–95, all children were counted under IDEA, Part B.

Learning from Inclusion

The inclusion of Girl Scouts with disabilities into groups or troops with nondisabled Girl Scouts has advantages for both groups of girls. Everyone will learn that she is more alike than she is different. The girls with disabilities learn to function in a group of nondisabled persons that is more like the world in which they will function as adults. They learn to use their assets and to compensate for their liabilities. They learn they can contribute to society.

Nondisabled girls learn to focus on what a person can do rather than on what a person cannot do. The nondisabled girls learn that each person is an individual. They learn not to stereotype people with disabilities, acquire accurate information about disabilities, and learn to identify the barriers in the physical, social, and emotional environment that limit the ability of people with disabilities to become part of society.

Adults in Girl Scouting can ensure that all the girls benefit. When the gains are weighed against the additional time and energy necessary, the benefits for all people involved far outweigh the investment made within the troop or group.

Chapter 2

Preparing Your Troop or Group

An important element in the success of integrating a Girl Scout with a disability into the troop or group is preparation—the time spent developing an understanding of the many facets of a disabling condition. Solid preparation will lead to a smoother and more rewarding experience.

While preparing to welcome a Girl Scout with a disability into your troop or group, keep in mind that you may already have a Girl Scout with a disabling condition in the troop. You may be unaware of the disability; indeed, the girl may have a disability that has not been identified by anyone.

As you make adaptations for the Girl Scout with a known disability, these changes may also help other girls in the troop or group who have minimal problems or unidentified problems to participate in the activities.

The girls in your troop or group may have already had some experience with persons with disabilities because of the integration of such students into the public schools. However, they will look to you, the leader, for your degree of acceptance of a Girl Scout with a disability. They will follow your lead in their reactions and behaviors.

1. PREPARING YOURSELF

The first step in preparing the troop or group is to prepare yourself—your attitudes and your degree of knowledge. If you have any fears, stereotyped beliefs, or inaccurate information, you may communicate these to the girls without saying a word. If you pity the Girl Scout with the disability, you will communicate this feeling to her as well as to the other troop or group members. If you resent making adaptations, it will be obvious to the girl with a disability as well as to the rest of the troop or group.

Attitudes

To evaluate your attitudes toward people with disabilities, ask yourself the following questions:

- Do I avoid eye contact when talking with people with disabilities?
- Do I speak for people with a speech or language impairment when they are capable of answering for themselves?
- Do I avoid touching people with disabilities?
- Do I hear myself saying, "She can't do that because she is disabled," before I have met the person?
- Do I avoid asking people with disabilities a question because I am afraid it will upset them?
- Do I feel sorry for people with disabilities?
- Do I find myself thinking of the disability before I think of the person?
- Do I find myself speaking of people with disabilities as a group? Example: "Blind people are good in music."

If you answer "yes" to any of these questions, you need to think about why you are answering this way. Your feelings may come from early associations with the disability. Perhaps as a child you saw an amputee in a wheelchair and, as a young child would do, you asked your parents, "Where is the rest of her leg?" Your parents or another adult responded with, "Be quiet and don't ask those questions! She might hear you." Or, as you looked to see where the leg was, your parents said, "Don't stare!" As a result, it may be difficult to look directly in the eyes of people with disabilities. As a child you may have heard myths and misinformation about

people with disabilities. For example, you may have heard that people who are blind have better hearing. With no other ideas about people with disabilities, you accepted such ideas as the truth.

As you discover the reasons for your feelings, you will be able to eliminate some of the myths you have learned about people with disabilities. With accurate information, you will be able to accept the Girl Scout with a disability as an individual.

Background Information

Another way of preparing yourself is to increase your knowledge of the disabling condition of your new troop or group member. It is important to have accurate information about the girl with a disability. The girl's family or the girl herself can give you this needed information. Her school is another source. Be certain to work closely with parents or guardians when obtaining this information. You will need parental release for girls whose school records contain confidential information.

Consider the following questions:
- What is the disability? What is the degree of disability?
- How much adaptation of the activities will be necessary?
- Are there medical or health considerations I need to be aware of, such as medication, diet, or physical needs?
- Is there a behavioral condition I need to be aware of, such as a limited ability to remember?
- Is there an environmental situation I need to be aware of, such as where the source of light should be located for a girl with a visual impairment to see best?

To learn more about the disability, you can locate a list of resources from your local library. The "Resource Information" section of this book also contains a listing of suggested reading material, as well as the names of organizations that can provide information.

2. PREPARING THE GIRLS

Before the arrival of the girl with a disability, it is important that the nondisabled girls in the troop or group learn more about disabilities and feel comfortable with people with disabilities.

For disabilities that interfere little with typical functioning, you may only need to give the minimum information needed for the girls to understand the condition. (Examples: learning disabilities, mental retardation, or chronic health conditions such as asthma, heart condition, or diabetes.)

If the disability is visible or interferes more greatly with typical functioning, more explanation may be needed. (Examples: blindness, deafness, physical disabilities, or autism.)

Listed below are suggested ways to introduce girls who do not have a disability to those who do.

1. Ask the troop or group members the same questions about attitudes that you asked yourself. Encourage the girls to discuss their answers and try to identify the reasons for their attitudes and feelings.

2. Have one or more persons with a disability visit the troop and talk about the disability. They can:
- Explain what they can and cannot do.
- Tell some unique things that have happened to them.
- Talk about how the disability came about.
- Explain what people do that helps them and what people do that does not help them.
- Discuss some of the barriers in the community that interfere with their activities, especially barriers that aren't physical.
- Talk about their feelings when they are faced with a barrier.

Following their talk, the visitors should set aside time for a question-and-answer period. It is crucial that the girls ask their own questions and that you do not screen those questions. Curiosity is natural and appropriate. You can help with phrasing to eliminate improper terms such as "fits," "dumb," "idiot," "retard," or "harelip," while still ensuring that girls are comfortable asking questions.

3. Find out about informative resources. For example, many local organizations and support groups have a video library. In addition, your public library can provide names and officers of these organizations. The "Resource Information" section of this book lists many organizations, as well as suggested titles.

4. The girls can read books about famous people with similar disabilities. Your local library as well as organizations associated with people with disabilities have suggested reading lists and information that can help you.

3. PREPARING THE MEETING ENVIRONMENT

For some disabling conditions the physical environment is not a barrier to participation in the group activities. The physical surroundings for girls with learning disabilities, mental retardation, hearing impairments, behavior disorders, and speech and language disorders may require no changes. However, for girls with physical disabilities and visual impairments, the physical environment may play a large role in determining the amount of participation in the activities.

Analysis of a Site

It is necessary to analyze the building, meeting room, and other parts of the physical environment where the troop or group meets. This analysis would be an excellent troop or group project. Whenever possible, include Girl Scouts with disabilities in doing the analysis.

1. Find out about your state or local guidelines for building accessibility. Contact your state bureau of vocational rehabilitation, or locate the address in the telephone directory under "State Offices."
2. Look at, measure, and take notes about potential barriers. The reproducible form on pages 10–11 is one guideline you can use.

If you are unsure of what is needed in the physical environment, ask someone from an organization for people with disabilities to attend a meeting and to assist the troop or group. However, it is important that you and the girls, as a group, do the evaluation of the physical environment.

4. INTRODUCING THE GIRL TO THE TROOP OR GROUP

When a girl with a disability enters the troop or group, you should treat all the girls equally. She may already know the other girls from school or the community. If not, when introducing the new girl to the troop or group members, make sure you say something that will help the girls identify with her, such as any traveling she has done or her grade in school. Do not specifically mention the disability as an identifying characteristic. However, do not avoid a discussion if the subject is mentioned. Additional suggestions are included in each chapter.

Helping the Girl with the Disability

In helping the Girl Scout with a disability, a balance should be struck: Do not give an excessive amount of help, but at the same time do provide essential assistance. Expect the girl with the disability to ask for assistance when she feels it is needed.

The girls and the leader should learn to ask if they can help, and respect the answer "no" when the girl with a disability wants to do the task alone. If we do most things for a girl so that she avoids failure, we also prevent her success. The other girls can learn specific things to do that are helpful. Specific ideas for helping the girl with a disability are given in each chapter. A good rule to follow is to remove the barriers or alter the project so the girl with a disability can participate. Do not complete the project for the girl.

The time and energy you spend preparing yourself, the girls, and the meeting environment will help the girl with a disability participate fully in the troop or group.

ANALYSIS OF A SITE

When analyzing any site, it is important to check all areas; one part may be accessible while another may not. Use the following questions as a guideline for planning activities that are accessible to everyone. If you think of other situations, add them to the ones here.

LOCATION

1. Is the site on a route for public transportation?
2. Does one accessible route connect all buildings and facilities on the site?
3. Are there reserved parking spaces for people with disabilities?
4. Are they near the entrance?
5. Are spaces at least 96 inches wide with a 60-inch adjacent access aisle?
6. Are there curb cuts so that people using wheelchairs, carriages, carts, etc., can enter and exit more easily?
7. Are there tactile markings in the sidewalks in front of the curbs to warn people who are blind?

ENTRANCES

8. Is there a ramp at the entrance to the building? Does it go out at least one foot for every inch it goes up?
9. Are all doorknobs to main doors 3 feet from the ground so that people in wheelchairs can reach them?
10. Are there handrails present?

HALLWAYS

11. Does the hallway allow at least 32 inches for one wheelchair to pass or 60 inches for two to pass?
12. Is the floor surface smooth enough for wheelchairs to travel comfortably? Is there enough difference in surfaces for people who are blind to get cues?
13. Are door openings at least 32 inches wide?
14. Are door numbers in Braille?
15. If there is an elevator, are floor numbers as well as up/down buttons in Braille? Are all buttons low enough for a person in a wheelchair to reach?

16. Can the water fountains be used by people in wheelchairs or by people with other mobility impairments?

17. Are fire alarms low enough to be reached by people in wheelchairs? Are the directions in Braille? Are they equipped with flashing lights so that people with hearing impairments can be warned?

BATHROOMS

18. Are bathrooms on an accessible pathway?
19. Are doors at least 32 inches wide?
20. Is there at least one stall with handrails that could be used comfortably by a person in a wheelchair?

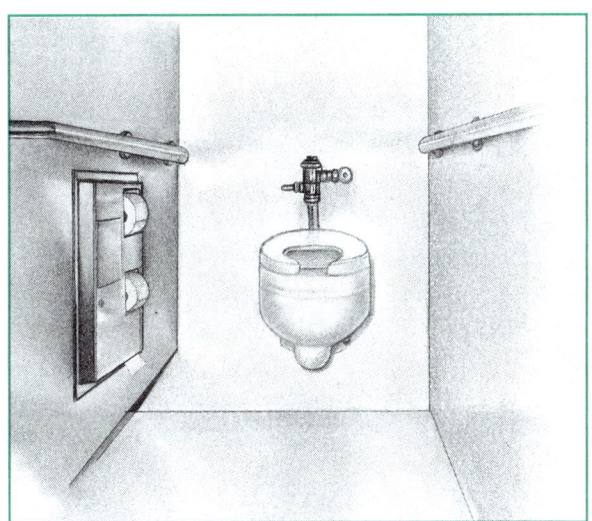

21. Do the stall doors swing out at least 90 degrees so that a wheelchair could move in and out freely?
22. Is there at least one counter and sink, and one soap and towel dispenser no higher than 34 inches?

TELEPHONES

23. Is there a clear ground space of at least 30 inches by 48 inches?
24. Is the height from floor to top no more than 48 inches?
25. Are there directions in Braille?

26. Is a TDD (telecommunications device for the deaf) available when needed?

MEETING ROOMS

27. How high are the shelves?
28. Are chairs and tables of an appropriate height? Can a wheelchair fit under at least one table, or can one be accommodated easily in an aisle?

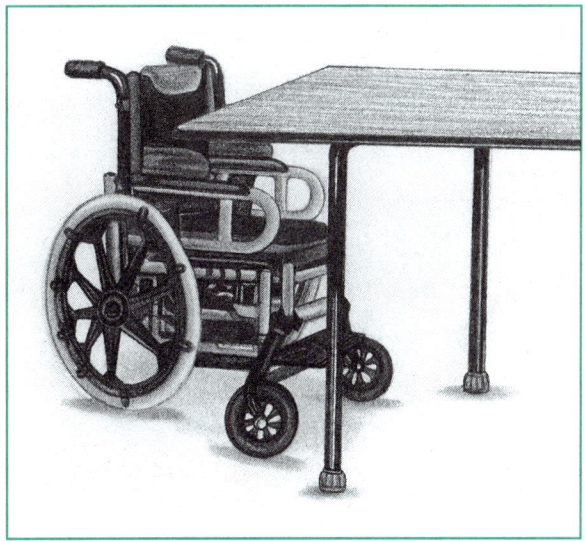

29. Do any cabinets or counters stick out into pathways?
30. Can all areas be seen without glare?
31. Have special materials and equipment that will be needed been identified? (Examples: handouts in large print, special pencils, special scissors.)

Source: Adapted from information in *Uniform Federal Accessibility Standards*, General Services Administration, Department of Defense, Department of Housing and Urban Development, and the U.S. Postal Service.

5. PREPARING THE ACTIVITIES

Because there is a wide range of abilities and conditions within each category of disability that may limit a girl's participation in the activities of the troop or group, it is impossible to present a specific list of adaptations that would be appropriate for all girls. What might be appropriate for one girl would not be appropriate for another girl with a similar disability. There are no recipes for working with girls with disabilities, and there are no recipes for designing activities for all girls' participation. However, here are some guidelines that can help the leader in making Girl Scouting meaningful to all girls.

Guidelines

When a girl with a disability joins a troop or group, it is important to evaluate all activities to see if they are appropriate for everyone in the troop or group and to identify any necessary adaptations. The following questions should be applied to each activity, whether it is a troop project or an individual patch requirement.

1. Do girls, rather than adults, provide the impetus for planning projects and activities?
2. Can all girls participate in the activity as it currently exists?
3. If all girls cannot participate in or be successful in all parts of an activity, what parts need adaptation? (Note that partial participation in an activity is much better than substituting a completely different activity, eliminating the activity, or not having a girl participate.)
4. Do adaptations need to be made in the entire project so all girls in the troop can participate in the activity?

After selecting a project, list the requirements or steps with the girl to determine if any adaptations are necessary.

Each chapter in this book contains a list of factors to consider when deciding about possible adaptations. In each chapter, you will also find suggestions for ways to alter an activity to help ensure success. As you check these lists, you will find that most activities need little or no adaptation.

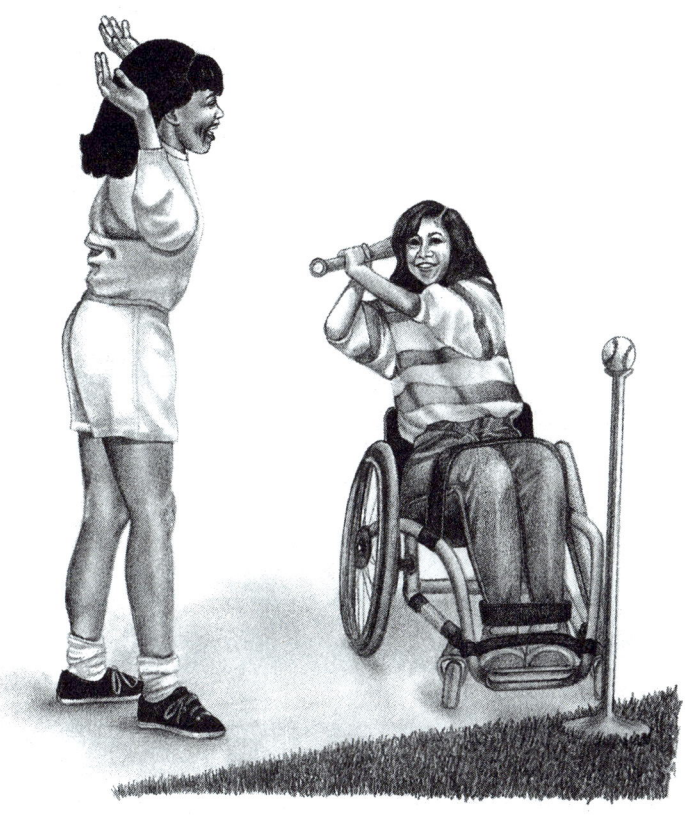

Examples of Adaptation

Below are examples of adaptations that easily can be made in Girl Scout activities. Remember that these are just examples and not the only adaptations possible. You and the girls you work with can use your creativity to develop new ideas.

Note that only partial versions of the activities are given. For the complete versions, see the *Brownie Girl Scout Handbook, Girl Scout Badges and Signs*, and *Interest Projects for Cadette and Senior Girl Scouts*.

BROWNIE GIRL SCOUT AGE LEVEL

SAMPLE ACTIVITY: *Brownie Girl Scout Handbook*, "People of the World" Try-It, "World Stories," page 243.

> Close your eyes and put your finger on a globe or world map. Use your imagination and tell a story about a girl your age who lives there.

Learning disabilities: Draw or cut out pictures if communication is difficult.

Communication disorders: Draw or cut out pictures or make some other kind of visual report if communication is difficult.

Mental retardation: Find out from her teacher or parents which countries would be appropriate. Use local or state maps as substitutions if necessary. Reports can be given through pictures or drawings if communication is difficult.

Behavior disorders: No change necessary.

Hearing impairments: No change necessary.

Visual impairments: Use a relief map or globe for locating the country.

Physical impairments: For girls who cannot use their hands, allow them to work with a buddy who will do the physical parts of the tasks.

JUNIOR GIRL SCOUT AGE LEVEL

SAMPLE ACTIVITY: *Girl Scout Badges and Signs*, Outdoor Fun badge, pages 211–212.

> 1. Help your troop, group, patrol, or family plan and carry out three different outings. They should each be one-half day or longer. Plan activities specific to the sites. Find out what types of equipment and facilities are already on each site. Then make a list of additional group and personal equipment you will need to take.

Mental retardation: Practice each part of the outing and make the list during the practice. The outing should remain simple and a limited number of materials should be necessary.

Plan a trip to a building or an area within walking distance of the meeting place. If you can obtain the equipment ahead of time, videotape the setting for the girls to review and become familiar with its appearance before the actual outing.

Visual impairments: Add an accessibility evaluation of the setting.

Physical and health impairments: Based on the abilities of the girl with a physical disability, evaluate the setting for accessibility.

All other disabilities: No change necessary.

2. With others, help plan, buy, pack, carry, prepare, and serve a different meal or snack for each of your three outings, such as one that requires no cooking, one that lets each person cook her own food, and one in which you cook for the group. Prepare a kaper chart for each meal or snack; include cleanup chores. For information on how to make sun tea and sun jam, see pages 247-248 in *Girl Scout Badges and Signs*.

Mental retardation: Rehearse all steps of the meal preparation before the outing. Keep the meal simple. Plan only one part of the meal that needs to be cooked, such as the dessert. Prepare some of the meal at the meeting place ahead of time.

Physical and health impairments: Check the setting for accessibility for girls with a physical disability. Make sure the menu reflects dietary needs. Bring any adaptive eating equipment the girl uses.

All other disabilities: No changes necessary.

3. Show that you can build a basic fire, prepare food on it, put it out, and leave the fire site "without a trace" of use. Remember to use only enough wood or charcoal to get your task done.

Communication disorders: No change necessary.

Learning disabilities, mental retardation, behavior disorders: Have a number of demonstrations and practices of each step of fire laying before actually lighting the fire.

Working in pairs with a nondisabled girl may ensure a more successful experience. Be sure that both girls actively participate in the activity.

Hearing impairments: No change necessary.

Visual impairments: Set up a model of a fire and fire circle so the girl with a visual impairment can become familiar through the sense of touch. This will allow the girl to practice laying a fire before she assembles, lights, and cleans up her own fire.

Physical disabilities and health impairments: The girl's physical abilities will determine the degree of assistance needed.

Using long fireplace matches will allow the girl to light the fire without physically moving—getting too close to the flames. Another idea is to tape the match to a dowel stick and then light the match from another, prelighted match. This allows the girl to light the fire from a safe distance.

Laying and building the basic A-frame fire in a raised charcoal cooker will allow a girl in a wheelchair to participate in the activity.

4. Help to plan, assemble, and pack a first aid kit that is appropriate for your outdoor activities. Demonstrate your knowledge of the uses of the items in the kit. Know prevention practices and first aid for burns and cuts.

Mental retardation: Use pictures showing the proper treatment.

Teach about simple and common injuries. Practice the first-aid procedure many times.

All other disabilities: No changes necessary.

CADETTE AND SENIOR GIRL SCOUT AGE LEVELS

Like the activities presented for younger girls, almost any activity for Cadette and Senior Girl Scouts can be adapted so that a girl with a disability can participate. Girls with and without disabilities should decide for themselves whether or not they would like to pursue for themselves particular interest projects, leadership projects, or the Silver and Gold Awards. All girls should choose activities which interest and challenge them, but which require as little adult input as possible. Girls with and without disabilities can suggest adaptations that make their activities more enjoyable.

SAMPLE ACTIVITY: Here are a few ideas for adapting a part of "Your Best Defense," from *Interest Projects for Cadette and Senior Girl Scouts*. Since girls with disabilities may have been protected from certain social situations, and are particularly vulnerable as they increase their independence, this interest project may provide them with invaluable skills.

> 1. Explore several philosophies of self defense. Learn about several martial arts such as karate, tae kwon do, jujitsu, and akido. Participate in classes or interview a martial arts master.

Learning disabilities: No changes necessary.

Communication disorders: Allow a girl to physically demonstrate different philosophies.

Mental retardation: If needed, a girl may use pictures or photographs.

Behavior disorders: Review the theories behind each martial arts philosophy and discuss how they may support concentration and self-control.

Hearing impairments: Consult with one or more martial arts experts who can demonstrate techniques that rely on senses other than hearing.

Visual impairments: Consult with one or more martial arts experts who can demonstrate techniques that rely on senses other than sight.

Physical disabilities: In addition to martial arts experts, consult with physical or occupational therapists on movements and methods to try.

> 2. Take a self-defense course designed for women and girls. Once you've completed the course, sponsor your own "mini" self-defense workshop for your friends and family, or for your Girl Scout troop or group.

All disabilities: Refer to the suggestions in Activity 1.

The development of adaptations can benefit everyone in the troop or group. All girls, both with and without disabilities, will have a number of strategies to use when they have to think quickly for self-defense.

> 3. Your body language and tone of voice can play a role in stopping a hostile or violent encounter from happening. Recite the following sentences—once with an angry voice and once again in a gentle manner. Think about the effect each version would have on the listener. How can you express your displeasure with someone without putting her or him on the defensive?
>
> "Shut the door now, please. I'm trying to study."
>
> "When are you going to return my sweater?"
>
> "I'm angry that you continue to lie to me."
>
> Make up three more emotionally charged discussions and role-play them.

Communication disorders: Let the girl change the words, take extra time, or choose some other method as long as it is one she would ordinarily use to communicate.

Hearing impairments: Let the girl choose a method of communication that is comfortable for her. If she uses sign language, have her develop strategies to use for those times when an interpreter will not be with her.

All other disabilities: No changes necessary.

Chapter 3

Simulating Disabilities

It is important for the girl and the adult members of the troop or group to understand the reactions of a person with a disability to the barriers in common activities. Getting dressed, listening to someone speak, reading, or moving around can be difficult if the environment is not altered in some way. Simulation activities are models or imitations of the disabling condition. Example: To perform an activity while blindfolded is simulation of blindness. Simulation activities offer the best way for the nondisabled Girl Scout to experience the feelings and frustrations that someone with a disability has when facing barriers.

Note that simulation of a disabling condition is a learning experience and should not be treated as a game. Also, simulation should not be viewed simply as a means of earning a patch. A simulation activity is meant to be a learning experience that leads to strategies for making Girl Scouting more inviting for girls with disabilities. Here are some directions:

Introduce the simulation activities to the troop or group by talking about people with disabilities whom the Girl Scouts know.

Have the girls discuss how they think people with disabilities do certain things. How does a person who is blind know how to buy clothes that match? How does a person in a wheelchair move in the snow? If a person with a learning disability cannot read, how can she or he vote in an election?

To get everyone involved, begin with a troop or group activity in which all of the members can participate. Continue with simulation activities that one person does in front of the group. This makes it possible for both the girl herself, and the group as a whole, to give reactions to the simulation. The last group of simulation activities should be done away from the meeting place or over an extended period of time. These activities give girls a better sense of how someone with a disability encounters a variety of everyday situations. Reactions may differ when the experience is longer than a few minutes.

You may want to try each activity yourself or have your assistant leader or a friend try the activities with you. This practice will help you to present the information smoothly and to anticipate reactions by the girls.

Directions are provided with each activity: Read all instructions very carefully and *follow them exactly*. Specific items needed for a simulation are listed with the activity. Special directions are noted. Try to create an atmosphere of tension and pressure, since this is what a girl with a disability would face.

1. TAKING A SPELLING TEST

(GROUP ACTIVITY)

HEARING IMPAIRMENTS

Supplies: cassette tape recorder
blank cassette tape
washcloth or towel
pencils and paper

Directions for Preparing the Materials

Make a tape recording of the words listed below as if you were calling out spelling words. Hold a washcloth over the microphone as you say the words. Do not repeat any of the words. Do not use the words in a sentence. Read the words slowly, allowing five seconds between each word.

Before using the tape recording with the troop or group, have your assistant leader or a friend take the spelling test. She should get from one to three words correct. If she gets more than three words correct, cover the microphone with the washcloth again, and re-record the words. The reason for using these particular words is that they sound very similar to other words.

Spelling words:

1. feel
2. cash
3. thumb
4. heat
5. rise
6. ledge
7. fish
8. shows
9. dread
10. juice

Directions for Using This Activity

Ask the Girl Scouts to number their papers from 1 to 10. Explain that this is an important test.

Play the tape. The girls should write the words they hear on their numbered paper. While the tape is playing, you should respond with little patience for questions or complaints. If a girl says that she cannot hear the words, respond with, "You are not listening," or "Listen harder!"

At the end of the tape, ask the Girl Scouts to check their papers while you read the correct words.

Have the girls tell how they felt during the testing. Did they give up trying to understand the words? Some of the girls may have given up and not finished the activity. Discuss why they did not finish. Did they feel angry during the test? In addition, have them discuss how they felt toward you when you would not help or would not repeat any of the words. Encourage them to talk about all of their feelings. They may express anger, fear, or feelings of failure. Then discuss how someone with a hearing impairment feels when she cannot hear a conversation. With this activity, encourage discussion about feelings and about how any person with a disability might feel in many different situations. Help the girls identify the barriers in the day-to-day life of a person with a hearing impairment.

The girls should end the discussion by listing some important things to remember when talking with a person who has a hearing impairment. Some suggestions can be found in Chapter Eight.

2. WRITING SENTENCES

(GROUP ACTIVITY)

HEARING IMPAIRMENTS

Supplies: cassette tape recorder
blank cassette tape
washcloth or towel
pencils and paper

Directions for Preparing the Materials

Follow the basic instructions for the previous activity, allowing 12 seconds between each sentence. Your assistant leader or friend should get from one to three words in each sentence correct. If more than three words in each sentence are correct, cover the microphone with the towel again and re-record the sentences.

Sentences:

1. I don't want to meet at the show tonight.
2. Put that lid back on the box.
3. How do you spell your name?
4. This hat should be put in the closet.
5. Where have you put the clothes this time?

Directions for Using This Activity

Follow the directions for the previous activity.

3. WRITING ON PAPER ON YOUR FOREHEAD

(GROUP ACTIVITY)

LEARNING DISABILITIES

Directions for Preparing the Materials

No special preparation necessary.

Directions for Using This Activity

Have each girl place a piece of paper on her forehead and write her name on that paper.

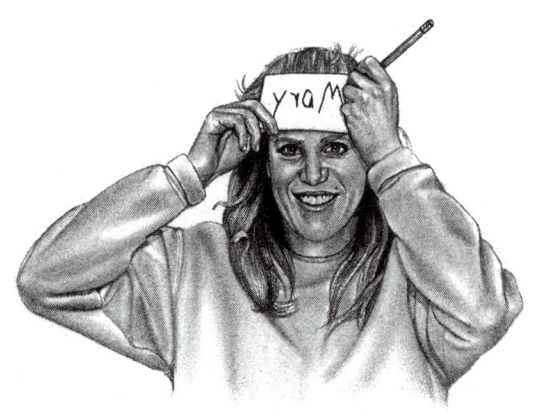

Some of the girls will write their names backwards. Lead a discussion on how the girls felt when they realized this later. Point out that the girls who wrote backwards did not realize, at the time, that they were writing backwards.

4. WRITING AND SWINGING YOUR FOOT

(GROUP ACTIVITY)

LEARNING DISABILITIES and ATTENTION DEFICIT DISORDERS

Directions for Preparing the Materials

No special preparation necessary.

Directions for Using This Activity

Ask the Girl Scouts to place their feet flat on the floor. Then have each girl lift her left foot and swing it in a counterclockwise motion.

At the same time that the girls are swinging their feet, ask them to write their names.

Following this activity, discuss how difficult it was to write well. In addition, discuss how the girls had to think hard about what they were doing even though it was a simple task.

Relate this to how difficult it is for a person with a learning disability or an attention deficit disorder to do many activities. During the discussion, focus on feelings of failure and frustration after not doing well on a simple task. Point out that although they do not usually have to swing their feet while writing, many girls are unable to keep still while working. Assist the troop or group in developing a list of ways to help someone or to alter an activity.

5. WRITING WITH PLIERS

(GROUP ACTIVITY)

PHYSICAL DISABILITIES

Supplies: pencils
paper
pliers (three or four pairs)

Directions for Preparing the Materials

No special preparation necessary.

Directions for Using This Activity

Ask each participant to hold her pencil with a pair of pliers when she writes. This activity can be a part of a troop or group project. Have the girls write for an extended period of time (three to five minutes).

Follow this activity with a discussion of the girls' feelings as they were struggling to write. Focus on their feelings of failure when they were having trouble and their feelings of success when they had accomplished part of the task.

6. TAKING A MATH TEST

(GROUP ACTIVITY)

MENTAL RETARDATION

The exercise shown here is appropriate for Junior, Cadette, and Senior Girl Scouts.

Supplies: math sheets
pencils and paper

Directions for Preparing the Materials

Make one copy of the math sheet for each girl (see next page).

Directions for Using This Activity

Tell the girls that they will be taking a timed test. Give each girl a pencil and the math exercise turned face down. Tell the girls to turn their paper over and begin the problems, working as fast as they can. Time them for about two to four minutes. At the end of the exercise, have the girls correct each other's papers.

Group the girls according to their number of correct answers. Name each group according to ability, such as battleships, steamships, and rowboats, or eagles, bluebirds, and crows. Treat the group that had very few correct answers as if they had not followed the directions and were not very smart.

Discuss how the girls felt when they found out some of their answers were wrong, perhaps because they had not followed the directions. How did they feel when they were put into groups according to ability? Lead the discussion toward how someone with mental retardation might feel when she makes a mistake. How might she feel when other people do not expect her to be successful?

In the discussion, develop strategies for helping someone with mental retardation without making her feel different.

19

MATH EXERCISE

In the following simple arithmetic exercise, a "+" sign means to multiply, a "÷" sign means to add, a "−" sign means to divide, and an "×" sign means to subtract.

Complete these problems following the above directions.

8 + 2 =   14 − 7 =

9 ÷ 3 =   6 × 5 =

4 × 3 =   8 + 3 =

6 − 2 =   7 × 2 =

9 − 3 =   9 + 2 =

7 × 4 =   8 ÷ 4 =

4 + 4 =   9 + 4 =

8 ÷ 4 =   1 − 1 =

12 × 2 =   8 + 7 =

9 − 1 =   16 ÷ 4 =

5 − 6 =   8 × 2 =

8 + 5 =   10 − 2 =

6 ÷ 6 =   15 × 3 =

7. PLACING COTTON IN YOUR EARS

(INDIVIDUAL ACTIVITY)

HEARING IMPAIRMENTS

Supplies: clean cotton balls, or a set of padded earphones from a stereo set
a scarf or tie

Directions for Preparing the Materials

No special preparation necessary.

Directions for Using This Activity

Have one girl gently place a cotton ball in the outer part of each ear and tie the scarf around her head to hold the cotton balls in place. As an alternative, you can place earphones over her ears.

The cotton balls or earphones should be used for part of the regular meeting.

Do nothing special for the girl. When she asks to have things repeated, just repeat what she didn't hear and remind her to listen carefully.

Do not let her copy from another girl's paper if you have a written activity.

When she interrupts, tell her to wait her turn.

Following this activity, lead a discussion on the girl's feelings during the activity. Discuss how she felt toward others—the leader, and the other Girl Scouts. This should lead into a discussion of the feelings of people with hearing impairments. The girls can develop a list of helpful hints for working with someone with a hearing loss.

8. WEARING DISTORTED GLASSES

(INDIVIDUAL ACTIVITY)

VISUAL IMPAIRMENTS

Supplies: plastic eye protectors, or safety glasses resembling eyeglasses
clear nail polish
red nail polish, or silver duct tape

Directions for Preparing the Materials

Purchase one or two pairs of inexpensive eye protectors used in factories. Use clear nail polish to cover each lens. On top of the clear nail polish put lines of red nail polish or strips of duct tape.

Directions for Using This Activity

Have one or two girls wear the special eye-protector glasses during an activity that requires use of the eyes, such as reading, writing, or walking.

Proceed with the meeting as if all of the girls can see very well. Make no changes in the activities until the girls with the eye protectors ask for help. Then give only limited help. Another way to respond is to do the entire task for the girl. Both responses are inappropriate ways of working with or giving aid to a person with a disability.

Following the activity, have a discussion about the feelings of the girls who used the eye protectors. How did they feel not knowing all that was taking place at the meeting?

As with the other simulation activities, develop a list of helpful hints for working with a person with a visual disability. Suggestions are provided in the chapter on visual impairments. It is important that the girls make the list. As the leader, you can guide the girls but do not give them the list.

9. WEARING A BLINDFOLD

(INDIVIDUAL ACTIVITY)

VISUAL IMPAIRMENTS

Supplies: blindfolds, fork, plate, hot dog, glass, beans, knife, water

Directions for Preparing the Materials

No special preparation necessary.

Directions for Using This Activity

Ask two or three girls to put on blindfolds.

Have the girls go to the bathroom, to the water fountain, or to another area in the building with a sighted guide to show the way.

Then ask another girl to put on a blindfold and try to do a troop or group activity that requires vision and use of the hands. Eating is a good activity to use. Another girl can give directions on the location of the food.

Following the activities, have the girls who were blindfolded talk about how they felt. The helpers can also explain how they felt. Have the blindfolded girls tell what was helpful and what was not helpful.

Develop a list of suggestions for guiding and for helping a person with a visual impairment.

10. USING MIRROR WRITING

(INDIVIDUAL ACTIVITY)

LEARNING DISABILITIES

Supplies: cardboard box
cardboard strips
mirror
silver duct tape
follow-the-dot sheet from a coloring book

Directions for Preparing the Materials

Two items will have to be made:

1. Obtain a cardboard box approximately 12 inches long, 12 inches wide, and 12 inches high. Completely remove one side of the box. On the side opposite this opening, cut out a narrow section five inches high and eight inches long.

2. Measure and cut a strip of cardboard 16 inches long and four inches wide. Bend the strip across at about seven inches to form a stand. With duct tape attach this stand to the back of a large, 8" × 8" mirror.

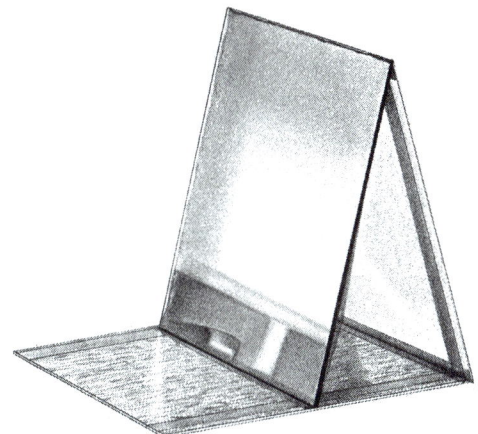

3. Make or purchase copies of follow-the-dot sheets. There should be one copy for each girl.

Directions for Using This Activity

The cardboard box has a large opening and a small opening. Place the box so that the small opening faces the girl.

Put the mirror on the stand in back of the large opening.

Place one piece of dot-to-dot paper under the cardboard box. The girl should place her hand through the small hole and write on the dot-to-dot paper. The girl will look over the top of the box and into the mirror. If the girl cannot see the paper in the mirror, adjust the mirror and the cardboard box until there is a good reflection. Next ask the girl to connect the dots. (The Girl Scout will not be able to control her hand to connect the dots.)

During the activity, make comments about the girl's quality of work and how messy her paper is.

After the task is completed, have the girl discuss how she felt during the activity. Ask about her feelings toward you while you were making comments. This should lead into a discussion of how a person with a learning disability might feel when trying a new task.

11. USING WHEELCHAIRS, CANES, AND CRUTCHES

(INDIVIDUAL ACTIVITY)

PHYSICAL DISABILITIES

Supplies: wheelchair
canes
crutches

Directions for Preparation

You will need to obtain a wheelchair, canes, and crutches from an organization for people with disabilities.

Directions for Using This Activity

Have the girls try to do everyday activities while in a wheelchair, or on crutches, or using a cane. Suggested activities are:

1. Go to the bathroom
2. Make a telephone call
3. Wash their hands
4. Make a sandwich
5. Get a drink of water

Following the activity, develop a list of places in the building that a person in a wheelchair cannot go.

Develop a list of simple things that a person with a disability would have difficulty doing.

Discuss what changes would have to be made to have a barrier-free building.

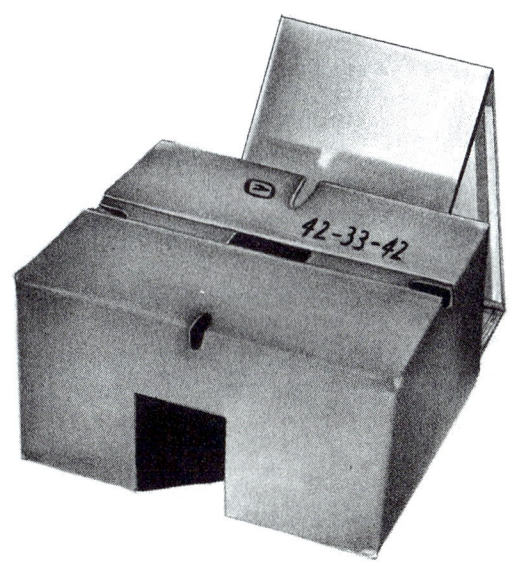

12. READING PARAGRAPHS

(SMALL GROUP IN FRONT OF THE LARGE GROUP)

LEARNING DISABILITIES

(Appropriate for Junior, Cadette, and Senior Girl Scouts)

Supplies: Two sets of the paragraphs shown on page 25–27, "The Lion" and "Alice"

Each set should have five or six copies of the distorted paragraph plus one copy of that paragraph in readable print.

Directions for Using This Activity

Hand out the clear paragraphs from "The Lion" to one girl, and the distorted copies to five or six other girls. Make sure the girls are not sitting close to each other. Also, make sure that no one can see the paper of the girl who is reading the good copy.

Start calling on the girls, one at a time, to read their paragraph out loud.

Rush the girls who are reading the distorted copies.

When they cannot read their paragraph, call on the girl with the good copy to read a sentence. Make sure you praise her and compare her ability to the other girls' abilities. You might say, "I wish everyone could read as well as _____," or "Thank you for being such a good reader."

After reading the paragraphs, discuss the girls' feelings. Be sure to focus on how the poor readers felt toward the good reader.

Compare this to how the person with a disability feels when a nondisabled person explains how to do an activity. Develop a list of things to remember about helping a Girl Scout with a learning disability.

After completing the first set of paragraphs, "The Lion," read the second set of paragraphs, "Alice," if you have enough time. You may find it better to do "Alice" at a later meeting. If you do read both paragraphs at the same meeting, plan other activities to separate the two readings.

THE LION

Four pro ther slive dina count ryf araw ay. The har vest was over.

The four prot hers ster tedf or ano ther coun try.

Thre eof the pr othe rskne wall kin bsof magic. On bro ther bid

n ot no maqic.
   w

ALICE

Alice was beginning to get very tired of sitting by her sister on the bank, and of having nothing to do; once or twice she had peeped into the book her sister was reading, but it had no pictures or conversations in it, "And what is the use of a book," thought Alice, "without pictures or conversations?"

THE LION

Four brothers lived in a country far away. The harvest was over. The four brothers started for another country.

Three of the brothers knew all kinds of magic. One brother did not know magic.

ALICE

Alice was beginning to get very tired of sitting by her sister on the bank, and of having nothing to do; once or twice she had peeped into the book her sister was reading, but it had no pictures or conversations in it, "and what is the use of a book," thought Alice, "without pictures or conversations?"

13. PUBLIC SPEAKING

(ONE PERSON IN FRONT OF THE GROUP)

COMMUNICATION DISORDERS

Supplies: metronome (can be borrowed from a music teacher)

Directions for Preparation

This activity should be tried first with an assistant leader or friend.

Directions for Using This Activity

Set the metronome at a fast speed.

Have one troop or group member talk with another girl or have her repeat something familiar such as the Pledge of Allegiance or the Girl Scout Promise to the rhythm of the metronome. The girl should recite, not read.

Each time the girl makes a mistake be sure to say, "Stop, and start over again!"

Following the activity, discuss how she felt when she was repeatedly corrected. Have her explain any feelings of anger or frustration. Ask the other Girl Scouts how they felt during the exercise.

14. BUTTONING A SHIRT

(ONE PERSON IN FRONT OF THE GROUP)

PHYSICAL DISABILITIES

Supplies: large shirt or blouse
roll of masking tape

Directions for Preparing the Materials

No special preparation necessary.

Directions for Using the Activity

Tape the girl's fingers of her right hand together with masking tape. Then tape the fingers of her left hand together. Make sure you include her thumb under the tape.

Have the girl put on the shirt and ask her to button it. While she is trying to button the shirt, be sure to rush her. Make statements like, "You are holding everyone up," or "Why does it take you so long?"

After completing the task, ask the girl how she felt during the exercise. Ask her how she felt toward you while you were rushing her. Also, ask the other Girl Scouts how they felt while the girl was trying to button the shirt. How did they feel toward you? What did they want to do? What could they have done if they had gone to the girl and assisted her?

Lead the discussion so the girls will realize that if they do things for people with disabilities, they send a message that these people are not able to do things for themselves. They should allow the person with the physical disability to complete the task without being rushed. Lead a discussion on how to let people with disabilities know they are accepted as individuals with their own strengths and weaknesses.

15. THREADING A NEEDLE

(ONE PERSON IN FRONT OF THE GROUP)

PHYSICAL DISABILITIES

Supplies: a bulky pair of socks, or a pair of mittens
needle and thread

Directions for Preparing the Materials

No special preparation necessary.

Directions for Using This Activity

Have the Girl Scout put the socks or mittens on her hands.

On a table place a needle with a small eye and a piece of thread that has been broken, not cut, from the spool of thread.

Ask the girl to pick up the needle and thread, and then to thread the needle. During the time the girl is trying, rush her and ask her why she cannot do better.

At some point, whether or not she has completed the task, ask her how she felt during the activity. Ask her about her feelings toward you. Try to get her to talk about any anger she might have felt.

Relate this to people with physical disabilities and how they might feel when attempting a task or when rushed during a task. You can discuss why the person with a physical disability might not want to try something new or might want to stay away from groups of people. You might lead a discussion on how the nondisabled Girl Scout can help a Girl Scout with a disability with a task without doing the task for her (example: offering a needle threader). Have the girls give suggestions on what they would do about a Girl Scout who is rushing a girl with a disability or making negative remarks about her.

Help the troop or group develop a list of suggestions for assisting the Girl Scout with a physical disability without doing the tasks for her.

CONCLUSION

The purpose of the foregoing activities is to help the troop or group experience what it is like to have a disabling condition. With better understanding, girls should have increased awareness of the barriers faced by people with disabilities when doing everyday tasks. Experiences during these activities can help in the development of strategies for including all girls in Girl Scouting.

Chapter 4

Learning Disabilities

The largest group of children with disabilities, over 51 percent, have been identified as learning disabled by public and parochial schools (see table on page 5).

A learning disability is a confusing impairment. A child with a learning disability looks like anyone else and has average to above-average ability to learn. People may not always recognize those who have learning disabilities because they behave inconsistently. One minute they seem to understand what is expected, and the next minute they seem confused about what to do. This confusion has led many people to inappropriately characterize them as lazy or disobedient children. What you, the leader, may notice in a girl with a learning disability is that she may learn some things quickly and easily yet may have trouble acquiring other skills. She seems to be capable of learning but has a great deal of difficulty understanding instructions or doing some tasks. Because of this difficulty, the girl experiences failure and in many cases stops trying to learn new skills or drops out of groups and activities. Many times the girl will experience coordination difficulties; she may have fine motor difficulty or may stumble and fall easily.

With a better understanding of learning disabilities, you will be better able to prevent a girl's feelings of failure and frustration. This will help the girl with a learning disability to feel successful, more confident, and happy to remain in the Girl Scout program.

MYTHS AND STEREOTYPES

Stereotypes are often applied to all people with a learning disability whether or not the characteristics are true. Example: "All learning-disabled children have trouble reading." It is true that some children with learning disabilities have trouble reading. However, many children with learning disabilities are good readers.

A myth is a belief about people with an impairment that is not true. Example: "Children with learning disabilities are lazy." While they may not attempt new tasks because they do not understand the directions or what is required, the desire to do the task is present. Or, they may have learned that it is better not to try rather than to try and to fail again and again.

Stereotypes and myths can prevent us from accepting people for their individual assets. Because of our beliefs, we expect a person to behave in a certain manner. We tend to look for this behavior and while doing so we miss all the wonderful things the person can do.

Here are some common myths and stereotypes concerning learning disabilities. People with learning disabilities:

- Are lazy.
- Are retarded. Can't learn.
- Are dumb.
- Try to be funny to get attention.
- Could learn if they would just try harder.
- Could do certain things if they would just practice enough.
- Do not pay attention.
- Have no self-discipline.
- Are disobedient.
- Should be excused from activities that are difficult.
- Should be allowed to disobey rules because they do not know how to follow rules.

CHARACTERISTICS

A Girl Scout with a learning disability is more like her nondisabled peers than she is different. Some specific characteristics that children with learning disabilities may show are discussed in this section.

By being aware of the areas of difficulty for a girl with a learning disability, you can adapt activities in ways that will promote success for all Girl Scouts in the troop or group. Remember that no girl will have all of the characteristics discussed. The degree to which each girl may show a characteristic is on a continuum. A girl may have a characteristic to a large degree or to a small degree.

EXAMPLE: CUTTING WITH SCISSORS				
Cannot manage scissors	Cuts with difficulty	Cuts with some difficulty	Cuts with ease	Cuts fine detail

⟵――――――――――――――――⟶

Some older girls with a learning disability may have learned strategies to compensate for their disability. They may have developed a variety of different techniques for accomplishing a task.

Motor Behavior

The child:

- May have difficulty buttoning, cutting, and writing. Her project or paper may appear messy and be torn, with the writing smeared. Her clothing may appear sloppy and be unbuttoned or buttoned improperly. This is due to an inability to control the small muscles in her hands, not to a lack of caring about her appearance.
- May have poor balance and posture. She may seem to trip over nothing or fall out of her seat. She may have trouble doing activities that require balance, such as walking in a straight line or standing on one foot. She may bump into things when it appears she has more than enough room to move.

- May have trouble moving to a rhythm. Dancing activities may be very difficult for her. It may appear she does not pay attention to the music. In reality she is paying attention but cannot control her body's motion to correspond to the music.
- May confuse left and right. She may make wrong turns when directions were just given. She may have difficulty moving about in a familiar setting.

Learning Ability

The child:

- May have trouble completing tasks. She may turn in unfinished projects and not realize they are incomplete. She may stop working or give up before finishing a project or an activity. This could be due to the frustration of not understanding the directions or of not being successful on a previous project.
- May have difficulty remembering facts and ideas that were just mentioned or discussed. It may seem she did not listen to what was said or done. Keep in mind that she was probably listening carefully and making an effort.
- May have trouble remembering the order of a list of items. She may remember the steps of the directions but will get the steps out of order. Example: Confusing the steps in mixing and baking a cake.
- May not seem to have her belongings organized. She may have her things dumped in her book bag but will not know where they are. She may have difficulty finding things that are right in front of her. Be patient and remember that she is looking for the necessary items.
- May have difficulty following oral directions. This could be for two reasons. Either she does not understand the directions or she does not remember the directions. It may appear to you that she was not listening. This is not true; she did listen but she did not remember.
- May misread words and therefore have difficulty understanding directions.
- May get confused when given more than one direction at a time.
- May have difficulty staying with one task. Before one task is completed, she will be doing something else.
- May seem easily distracted. She may be bothered by sights and sounds that do not seem to disturb others. She may go to the window to see the source of a sound or to the door to see who just passed. If another Girl Scout begins a new project, the Girl Scout with a learning disability may stop what she is doing to go see the new activity.
- May have difficulty making decisions. She may want you to make choices for her. Or, she may wait until others have chosen and then make the same choice.
- May be impulsive. Often she cannot determine the consequences of her behavior. She may start a task without waiting for the directions, or she may rush into a situation without thinking of the outcome. She may also blurt out a comment unrelated to the present activity simply because she thought of it.
- May have a poor sense of time. She may have little understanding of the length of time in a minute or an hour. She may have difficulty judging how long it will take to complete a task.
- May guess at answers to questions that require remembering information that is stored in the memory.

Communication Ability

The child:

- May be able to explain something out loud but not in writing. Another girl may be able to explain something in writing but not out loud.
- May be able to speak with a great deal of ease and clarity but have difficulty reading.
- May be able to demonstrate an idea or task but have difficulty explaining that idea or task.
- May have difficulty expressing her thoughts. When she is talking, her ideas may seem scattered. Her answers may not seem to relate to the questions or subject matter. For example, she may answer a question about her Girl Scout project with information about her schoolwork.

- May confuse letters or numbers that look similar. She may replace "b" with a "d" or "w" with an "m," a "3" with an "8" or "6" with a "9."
- May have difficulty spelling. Words that seem easy to spell may be misspelled. She may not be able to tell which words are correct and which words are incorrect. Words may be spelled correctly one day and incorrectly another day.

Emotional Behavior

The child:

- May have mood swings. One minute she seems to be working happily and the next minute she may burst into tears for no apparent reason.
- May have a poor self-concept and make negative remarks about herself. Because she has had difficulty doing some activities, she may not feel successful doing any activities. She may use "I can't do that!" many times.

Social Behavior

The child:

- May need to ask frequently if her work is correct. She may be very unsure of what to do and may ask you many times to check if her project is correct.
- May have difficulty developing friendships. She may not understand how to be a friend.
- May try to draw attention away from her learning problem by being disruptive when she is having difficulty.

ADAPTATIONS FOR GIRLS WITH LEARNING DISABILITIES

The following adaptations for girls with learning disabilities focus on setting the environment for maximum learning and participation.

Supportive Behavior

It is important for you to be supportive of and show encouragement to the Girl Scout with a learning disability.

1. From the beginning, avoid labeling the girl by her disability. This can defeat the entire purpose of inclusion.
2. Keep your voice at an even pitch when you speak.
3. Praise the little steps made by a girl with a learning disability. Do not wait until the end of the project to compliment her work.
4. Quietly assist the girl when assistance is needed or requested.
5. Focus on what is right, not what is wrong.
6. Be supportive of the girl with a learning disability during games and activities that are difficult for her. Reinforce her efforts and participation. However, do not overdo your support, as this will draw attention to the disability.

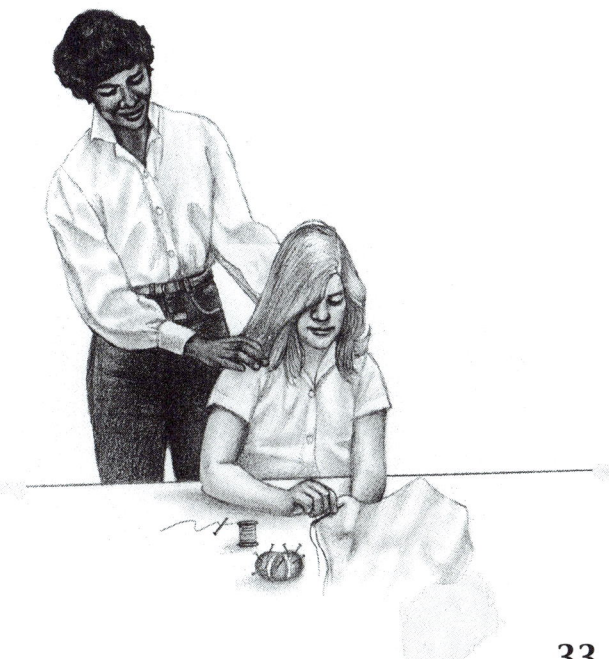

33

7. Carefully select any help given by a peer. Make sure the girl is sensitive to the abilities and limitations of the child with a learning disability.

8. When incomplete projects and tasks must be returned to her for completion, quietly point out the incomplete portion. Remember that the Girl Scout with a learning disability often does not know the project is incomplete.

9. Avoid conditions that may cause embarrassment to the girl. Do not use material that is inappropriate for her age level. If she has a reading problem, do not use material written for younger girls. Audiotaped versions of Girl Scout resources might be used, or have someone tape your own materials.

10. When the Girl Scout with a learning disability stops working on a project, quietly remind her of the current activity. Go by her work area and point to the next step to be completed. If she has wandered away from her work space, go to her and firmly take her back to the task. When you and the girl build a good working relationship, you will be able to use reminders without saying a word.

Communication

The following suggestions may be helpful when communicating with a girl with a learning disability.

1. Wait until the Girl Scout with a learning disability is ready to begin before you start explaining something or giving directions. Look directly at the girl and establish eye contact. Then begin to give directions to the troop or group.

2. Give directions in steps and number each step. Present no more than three steps of the directions at one time. When these steps have been completed, present the next set of steps. Give brief and specific directions that take a short period of time to complete.

3. Give directions both orally and in writing.

4. Make sure the girl with a learning disability understands what is to be done before she begins. After giving the directions to the troop or group, have the girl quietly repeat the directions to you or have her demonstrate the directions for you. Occasionally have everyone repeat the directions. This may help other troop or group members to remember the directions.

5. If the Girl Scout with a learning disability does not understand, say the directions in another way or in a simpler form. Do not repeat the directions using the same words.

6. Use concrete rather than abstract examples when explaining something. Concrete example: Being able to shop where you want. Abstract example: Being able to have an opinion.

7. Use very exact communication. Do not expect the Girl Scout with a learning disability to understand subtle comments. If you expect the troop or group to wait at a certain place, mention the specific place to wait. Do not give a general location.

8. When the girl with a learning disability cannot find an item that seems easy for you to locate, remember that she is looking but does not see the item. Give the girl specific directions on how to locate the missing item but do not go after it for her. Example: "Look on top of the book."

Presentation of Materials and Activities

The following ideas can be helpful in presenting activities to a Girl Scout with a learning disability.

1. When a great deal of written material is being presented, use a highlighter pen to emphasize the important parts. This will help the girl know where to focus her attention and what should be remembered.

2. Color-code steps and items to help organize the activity. Place a certain colored mark on things that are to be done first, another colored mark on things that are to be done second, and so forth.

3. Before a trip, list some very specific things for her to look for while traveling. Example: If you are attending a court that is in session, you might have her notice where the judge sits, who asks the questions, and who answers the questions.
4. Give the girl with a learning disability an outline or format for the written sections of a project. Leave blanks for the girl to fill in with the missing information, or give her specific questions to be answered.
5. Suggest the girl use the audiotape version of her handbook if she has difficulty reading (see "Resource Information," page 103).
6. Provide printed reminders if she needs them. She may need the steps of a project listed on a card placed in front of her.

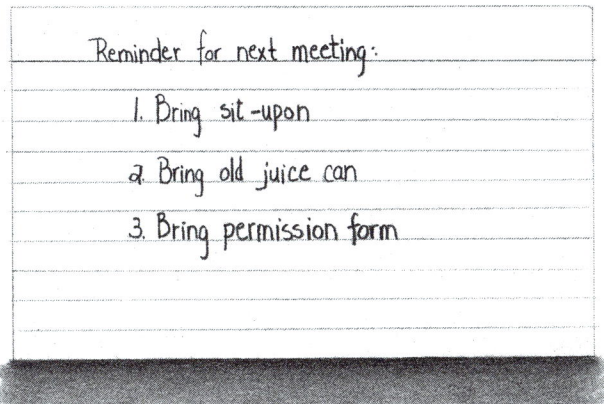

7. Divide work into small steps or sections. Give only one step or section at a time. When a girl with a learning disability sees a long project, she may give up. Seeing small steps is more encouraging. Showing her how many steps she has completed may encourage her to complete the activity.
8. Limit the choices. Have the girl with a learning disability choose between two things rather than many things. Example: "You may use either the red paper or the blue paper."
9. Follow a set routine during meetings. This helps the girl with a learning disability know what is expected. When it is necessary to change the routine, let her know about the change ahead of time.
10. Structure the material for the girl with a learning disability. For example, put the items in the order that they will be used.
11. If possible, provide a model or an example of what is to be done. Use direct experience when introducing something new. The girl with a learning disability should be able to see and touch the example as well as hear the directions for the activity.
12. Use diagrams and pictures when possible. This gives the girl with a learning disability the opportunity to see what is to be done as well as to hear you tell what is to be done.

Adaptation of Materials and Activities

The following suggestions give some alternatives in adapting materials and activities.

1. Give the Girl Scout with a learning disability extra time to complete projects. Allow her to work slowly.
2. When an activity includes designing a project, give the girl with a learning disability some ideas. In addition, you might have her describe the activity and tell how the finished project will look.
3. Select games that allow for a variety of ways to participate. Example: Running relays to the end of the room while balancing a beanbag somewhere on the body. One girl could balance the beanbag on her hand, and another girl could balance it on her head. This allows each girl to select her own way to be successful.
4. For activities that require using scissors, provide assistance if it appears the project may be ruined. However, do not do all of the cutting for the girl. Only help cut around the difficult parts.
5. The Girl Scout with a learning disability may need additional practice. Allow time for the girl to rehearse an activity as many times as necessary.
6. When the meeting includes rhythm activities, give the girl verbal signals. Have her count to herself or give her some words to help trigger a certain action or

response. For younger girls, an example would be to put a small red dot on her right hand. You could then say "red" when she is to use her right hand or foot.

7. Encourage the girl with a learning disability to do some activities orally rather than in writing. This oral project can be tape recorded and then put into a written report.

8. Encourage the girl with a learning disability to use a pencil instead of a pen. When the project is complete, she can copy it in ink.

9. Give the girl with a learning disability a choice between cursive writing and printing.

10. For a child who has a problem holding a thin pencil to write, use either a pencil gripper or a triangular-shaped pencil. A pencil gripper can be purchased at most stationery stores for under a dollar.

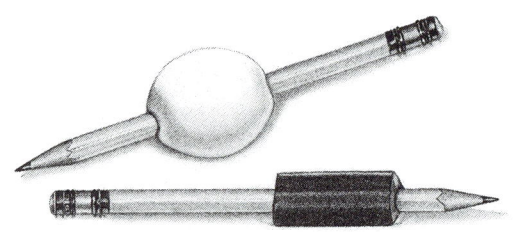

Memory and Organizational Skills

Use the following suggestions to help the girl with a learning disability remember routine things and organize her work space.

1. Have her keep a reminder list of things she is to bring to the next meeting or of things she is to do between the meetings.

2. Give suggestions to help the girl remember. Assist her in developing a pattern, such as putting all lists in alphabetical order.

3. Have the girl repeat to herself or to you any items to be remembered.

4. While working on a project, limit the number of items in the girl's work area. Only the materials she will use on one step of a project should be in front of her.

5. Have the girl work in a quiet area. This applies to both things she sees and hears. Noise and clutter may distract her. What may seem like an attractive room can be distracting for the girl with a learning disability.

6. Help her to keep her work organized. Go by her work station and quietly assist her in putting things into a pattern or into proper work order.

Behavior

1. Do not expect the girl with a learning disability to understand social behavior. You will have to explain what behavior is expected. Be firm when explaining the social behavior but do not make it sound like a punishment.

2. Let the girl know quietly and privately when her behavior is not appropriate and describe what behavior is expected. Remember to let the girl know when her behavior is appropriate.

3. Give alternatives for immature or inappropriate behavior. Do not belittle or embarrass the girl. Be firm, calm, and specific in explaining what behavior is expected.

4. Give the girl with a learning disability a chance to move around the room if she seems to be inattentive or distracted. Change the activities from quiet to active; allow the girl to go on errands.

5. Before a trip or a special event, be very exact in explaining what behavior is expected. Let the girl know when she is to listen and when she is to ask questions. If she forgets, quietly touch her arm to remind her.

6. Let the girl know when the activity is about to change. "In five minutes, we are going to _____." Do not switch to another activity without preparing the girl for the change.

7. Be sure to notice the activities the girl does well. By encouraging the girl with the learning disability to participate in such activities, you will help to build her self-esteem and her leadership abilities.

FAMOUS PEOPLE

Many famous people have been identified as having learning disabilities; a few are listed below. You can add to this list.

Harry Anderson, *comedian, actor*
Cher, *singer, actress*
Agatha Christie, *author*
Sir Winston Churchill, *British prime minister*
Tom Cruise, *actor*
Leonardo da Vinci, *artist*
Thomas Edison, *inventor*
Albert Einstein, *scientist*
Tracy Gold, *actress*
Whoopi Goldberg, *entertainer*
Bruce Jenner, *Olympic athlete*
Jay Leno, *comedian*
Greg Louganis, *Olympic athlete*
Amy Lowell, *poet*
Dexter Manley, *football player*
Pablo Picasso, *artist*
Woodrow Wilson, *U.S. President*

Chapter 5

Communication Disorders

One of the most meaningful parts of our life is our ability to communicate with other people. In communicating with others, we exchange our joys and sadnesses, our wants and needs, and we fulfill our thirst for knowledge through the exchange of ideas. Communication and interaction with others help to meet our basic need for contact with people.

The most common way of communicating our thoughts and ideas is through the use of speech and language. Speech refers to the sounds we use when communicating our thoughts and ideas. Language is the formation of thoughts and ideas into meaningful parts such as sentences and phrases.

For some people, these processes do not develop typically. When there is difficulty in communicating, whether it involves speech or language, it affects all parts of a person's life: academic, social, emotional, and vocational. This disability is called a communication disorder.

Note that some speech and language problems may relate to a hearing loss. Sometimes a girl with a hearing impairment will also have a speech or language problem. Other causes of speech and language disorders include mental retardation, brain injury, neurological disorders, physical impairments, or vocal abuse. Often the cause is unknown.

CLASSIFICATIONS

Communication disorders are classified into two large groups: speech disorders and language disorders.

Speech Disorders

Speech disorders involve the way we make the sounds of words. Following are the three most common speech disorders.

Articulation errors: Changing the sounds through substitution, omission, distortion, or addition. Examples of articulation errors are "wabbit" for "rabbit" and "shled" for "sled."

Dysfluency: Interruption of the flow or rhythm of speech. An example is stuttering.

Voice disorders: Types of speech sounds that interfere with understanding of the intended message. A disorder may be in the area of pitch, volume, or quality. The leader might hear a voice that is too high, too loud, or too soft. Extreme nasal, raspy, or monotone voices are also considered voice disorders.

Another problem that interferes with producing sounds of speech is the cleft lip or cleft palate. When the lip and the palate do not close properly during development of the nose and mouth before birth, air escaping through the nasal passage creates a nasal quality to the speech. Through advances in technology, the majority of children with cleft lips and palates have surgical correction early in life. Only the girl with a very severe cleft lip or cleft palate will be recognized or need any kind of adaptation.

Language Disorders

Language disorders relate to the way ideas are understood or expressed. Girls with language disorders may have both verbal and nonverbal problems with grammar, vocabulary, and following directions. They may see or hear a word and not know what it means, or they may not be able to express themselves so that others can understand them. A language disorder may be related to other disabilities such as mental retardation, traumatic brain injury, or learning disabilities, or may be the only disability a girl has.

MYTHS AND STEREOTYPES

Many myths and stereotypes are still associated with communication disorders, even though a number of well-known people in history have had such disorders. Following are some of the common myths and stereotypes related to communication disorders.

- People with speech and language problems are dumb.
- Communication disorders are learned or inherited from parents.
- All children grow out of their speech problems.
- People who stutter should not speak in public.
- People who stutter have emotional problems.

Unfortunately, people with communication disorders often are still expected to have some of these stereotypical characteristics and are not viewed as unique individuals. It is important that you, as the leader, separate myths or stereotypes from accurate information.

CHARACTERISTICS

Remember that a girl with a speech disorder is more like other girls the same age than different from them. She can participate in all troop or group activities with only minor adaptations.

The girl with a language problem may have difficulty understanding and producing meaningful sentences and phrases. You may observe some of the following characteristics.

Motor Behavior

The child:

- May have distorted facial expressions as she attempts to communicate.
- May have a tense body while trying to produce sounds or words.

Communication Ability

The child:

- May avoid situations where she has to speak.
- May use "baby talk" because she has difficulty expressing ideas.
- May not speak in complete sentences.
- May use immature grammar—for example, "Me go to the store."
- May have difficulty understanding the meaning of what is being said.
- May not understand the meaning of long and complicated sentences.
- May not understand advanced or abstract ideas.

Emotional Behavior

The child:

- May have a greater speech or language problem in tense situations.
- May not feel self-confident and may make negative statements about herself.

Social Behavior

The child:

- May feel uncomfortable interacting with other girls.
- May feel isolated or disliked and not want to participate in group activities.

ADAPTATIONS FOR GIRLS WITH COMMUNICATION DISORDERS

Adaptations for Girl Scouts with communication disorders focus on building an atmosphere of acceptance and encouragement. The objective is to establish a relaxed and comfortable environment.

Supportive Behavior

As the leader, you can help the girl with a communication disorder to become an active, happy member of the troop or group.

1. Be a role model by using appropriate speech and language; avoid baby talk, slang, or incomplete sentences.
2. When the girl is speaking, give her your complete attention. Remember, you are also demonstrating good listening skills for the other Girl Scouts. As the leader, you try to instill trust, confidence, and sound values. If you do not give full attention, you convey that what this girl has to say is not important; you further instill inappropriate responses in the other troop or group members.
3. Speech and language errors should not be criticized or mimicked by the leader or by other Girl Scouts.
4. Do not mention the communication disorder when referring to the girl; try to reduce all the girls' awareness of the problem by not drawing attention to it. However, do not ignore the problem or deny that it exists.
5. Do not correct the girl's speech or language errors; simply rephrase the statement using the correct sound or word. If the girl says, "I have a wed wabbit," respond with "I am glad you have a red rabbit." Or, if she says, "I wented to the store," you could reply, "What did you get when you went to the store?"

Communication

You can assist the girl who is having difficulty communicating by remembering the following.

1. When a girl with a communication disorder is speaking, maintain continuous eye contact with her. This shows respect and interest.
2. Encourage any attempts at oral communication.
3. Give the girl frequent opportunities to speak. Begin with informal conversation and advance to group discussion. It is extremely important that you do not speak for the girl.
4. Encourage the girl to ask for the meanings of words she does not understand.
5. When she has difficulty finding the correct word to use, do not be too quick to supply any missing words. When it is necessary to assist her, do so in a quiet and gentle way.
6. If the girl is stuttering, do not fill in the word she is attempting to say. Give her time to say the word or rephrase the sentence. Do not tell her to stop and start over again.
7. When necessary, provide information in shorter, less complex sentences for the girl.
8. When there seems to be confusion in understanding the information given, rephrase using other words.
9. When a new idea is introduced, make sure your explanation is simple and clear. Any new words relating to the idea or event should include a definition. Do not assume all members of the troop or group will know the meanings of the new words.
10. When giving directions, try one or more of the following:
    - Pause between steps.
    - Number the steps.
    - Use short, simple sentences. However, do not use baby talk and do not belittle the girl.
    - Have her repeat the directions to you.
11. When a Girl Scout with a communication disorder finds it difficult to express herself, use questions that require a yes, no, or one-word answer rather than questions which require her to create her own answer. As she becomes more comfortable with you, the other girls, and the troop or group activities, ask questions which require longer answers.

Presentation of Materials and Activities

Consider the following suggestions when presenting activities and materials.

1. As the leader, you should not decide whether the Girl Scout with a speech or language problem is going to speak in front of the troop or group. The choice should be hers.
2. For the child with a language disorder, be aware of words that are hard to define—namely, action words and words that explain location such as "under," "over," "near," and "beside." It may be helpful to use a picture or to physically demonstrate the meanings of these words.

Adaptation of Materials and Activities

Following are ideas to help you adapt materials and activities for a Girl Scout with a communication disorder.

1. People rarely stutter while singing or speaking in unison. This means that singing or reciting can be a very successful activity for the girl who stutters.
2. The girl who stutters will rarely have a communication problem while performing in a skit or play using puppets or masks. These are good activities for troop and group projects, since all girls can participate.

Behavior

It is important to provide a comfortable meeting environment.

1. Try to reduce tension in situations that appear to increase stuttering. This can be accomplished by your maintaining a calm, relaxed manner while respecting each girl as an individual.
2. Encourage speaking when all is going well. A good time to encourage the girl to interact with the other troop or group members is during relaxed, enjoyable activities.
3. The child may become frustrated when she cannot find the correct word and may lose control of her emotions. Remain calm and take the attention away from her by focusing attention on another activity.
4. Encourage her to work in a small group with girls who show good speech and language patterns.

FAMOUS PEOPLE

People with communication disorders can become successful in whatever vocation or job they choose. Listed below are some famous people who have or had speech or language disorders.

Aristotle, *philosopher*
Sir Winston Churchill, *British prime minister*
King George VI of England
Annie Glenn, *lecturer*
Thomas Jefferson, *U.S. President*
James Earl Jones, *actor*
Patricia Neal, *actress*
Sir Isaac Newton, *scientist*
Carly Simon, *singer*
Mel Tillis, *singer*

Chapter 6

Mental Retardation (DEVELOPMENTAL DELAY)

Mental retardation (also called developmental delay) is a comprehensive disability that affects not only academic and language learning but also the development of social and emotional skills. Girls classified as having mental retardation have the ability to learn, but they learn more slowly than children with average ability. Most people with mental retardation (about 87 percent) will have mild difficulties and as adults will live independently. In most circumstances, they will not be considered as having mental retardation. The other 13 percent of those with mental retardation will have more serious limitations, but with appropriate supports they can participate fully in community life.

A DEFINITION OF MENTAL RETARDATION

According to the American Association of Mental Retardation (AAMR), the definition of mental retardation is based on three criteria: intellectual functioning (IQ) is below 70–75; significant limitations in adaptive skills are present in two or more areas; and the condition occurs during the developmental period (age 18 or less). All three parts of the definition must be present for a girl to be identified as having mental retardation (AAMR, 1992).

A commonly misunderstood term used with mental retardation is mental age. The term mental age is only used in intelligence testing. It means that someone scored the same number of correct responses on an IQ test as the average person of that age. Using this term to infer that a person has the mental capabilities of someone younger is incorrect. It only relates to an IQ score, and does not indicate adaptive skills or one's ability to participate in the community (AAMR, 1992).

The AAMR considers nine areas in determining adaptive skills: communication, self-care, home living, social, self-direction, health and safety, community use and work, leisure and work, and functional academics.

Examples of these skills are:

- *Communication skills:* Greeting other people.
- *Self-care skills:* Dressing herself.
- *Home living skills:* Preparing a snack or meal for self and friends.
- *Social skills:* Eating in a restaurant.
- *Self-direction skills:* Cleaning one's room without prompting or supervision.
- *Health and safety skills:* Ability to find a police officer in an emergency.
- *Community use and work skills:* Paid employment and/or meaningful volunteer work.
- *Leisure and work skills:* Being part of a team.
- *Functional academic skills:* Ability to write a check and balance a checkbook.

THE INCLUSION OF GIRLS WITH MENTAL RETARDATION IN GIRL SCOUTING

As an organization committed to the development of all girls, Girl Scouting offers the ideal setting for girls with mental retardation to develop friendships as well as skills. Inclusive recreational and leisure activities are essential to the quality of life for people with mental retardation. By participating in activities appropriate to their chronological age, and along with their nondisabled peers, they are better able to learn the skills and attitudes needed in everyday life (*The Arc*, 1992).

Therefore, girls with mental retardation should be registered as closely as possible to their chronological age. They wear the uniform of that age level. Adaptations should be made of the ongoing activities of the age level to which the troop belongs. When girls reach the age of 18 or complete high school or its equivalent, they move into an adult membership category. Young women who have mental retardation may, if they wish, retain their girl membership through their 21st year if they are still in high school, and then move into an adult category.

MYTHS AND STEREOTYPES

As the leader of the troop or group, you can work to eliminate any of the following myths and stereotypes by providing correct information.

Some commonly held misconceptions about people with mental retardation are that they:

- Are dangerous.
- Cannot hold a job.
- Should do everything based on their "mental age."
- Are all alike.
- Should not have children because they do not know how to properly care for children.
- Will have children with mental retardation.
- Should not be left alone because they may hurt themselves.
- Commit more crimes than those without mental retardation.
- Should not be hired to work because the company's insurance rates will go up.
- Should not be hired because other company employees would have to help do most of their work.
- Should be avoided because you can catch mental retardation.
- Cannot be expected to learn age-appropriate behavior, so should be excused from it.
- Do not have the thoughts and feelings that others their age might have.
- Are "forever children."

CHARACTERISTICS

Since each girl will have different adaptive skills, each will have different characteristics. Some may not be obvious.

Motor Behavior

The child:

- May have difficulty with activities requiring large muscle coordination. Skills such as running and walking may be mastered more slowly than is the case with other girls.
- May be delayed in developing fine motor skills such as writing, cutting, and using tools with the nondominant hand. Her coordination when using hand tools may seem immature and awkward.
- May have poor eye-hand coordination. She may have difficulty threading a needle or accomplishing a task where the hands and eyes must work together.

Learning Ability

The child:

- May need to practice many times before learning a skill.
- May have difficulty learning abstract concepts. Concepts such as freedom or loyalty, for example, may be difficult for the girl with mental retardation to understand without concrete examples.
- May have difficulty applying what she learned in one setting to what she needs to use for another setting. Example: She may learn to raise her hand to ask a question but not know to raise her hand to answer a question.
- May be easily distracted by sights and noises in the environment. When two activities take place simultaneously, the girl may have difficulty concentrating on either activity.
- May seem hesitant about learning new tasks because of previous failures. She may avoid failure by not making an effort.

- May have difficulty with memory retention. She may seem to forget information from one day to the next day. Also, she may have difficulty remembering the sequence of information.
- May have difficulty reading. Her reading level may be below that of other girls her age.
- May have difficulty following directions, particularly if too many steps are presented at once. She may not complete a project or she may do the steps of the project out of order.
- May repeat a behavior or skill more times than is necessary. She may learn a skill and, upon realizing it is accepted as correct, may perform the same skill over and over. For example: When properly cutting an item from fabric for a project, she may continue to cut identical items until she is told to stop. She is concentrating on the cutting rather than on the end result.
- May not understand directions when there are many steps or when the steps are dependent on each other. For example:
  1. Draw a large pine tree on a hill.
  2. Draw a red bird in the middle of the tree.
  3. Draw a small worm in the mouth of the bird.

  If Step 1 is not correct, all the other steps will be incorrect.
- May have difficulty with self-directed material. Any task designed for independent work may be difficult.
- May perform below average in academic subjects such as arithmetic, spelling, writing, science, and social studies. Her ability in subjects such as art, music, and physical education may vary from below average to above average.
- May take longer to complete a task. She may work at a slower pace than other girls the same age.
- May be immature in her reasoning and judgment. This may be due to her disability, but may be influenced by her lack of social interaction with nondisabled peers.
- May have difficulty identifying common patterns such as styles of clothing or types of buildings. She may have difficulty seeing likenesses and differences in objects.

Communication Ability

The child:

- May not comprehend the meaning of what other children her age are saying.
- May have difficulty understanding a long and complex sentence. She may not recognize the most important part of the sentence.
- May have difficulty paying attention. Three of the most common reasons for this lack of attention are:
  1. She may have difficulty focusing on what is important.
  2. She may not understand what is being done.
  3. She may have a short attention span.

- May seem unable to recognize identifying cues. The girl may use a stray pencil mark to identify a page rather than using the page number.
- May have difficulty expressing ideas. Her thoughts and ideas may not be clearly stated and may be difficult for others to understand.
- May miss the point of jokes or riddles, since these generally require an understanding of language, and the language development of the girl may be delayed.

Emotional Behavior

The child:

- May become easily frustrated when attempting a new task. She may give up quickly or destroy her project when she feels she is not doing well.
- May not be able to deal with her emotions as well as might be expected considering her age and experience.
- May seem afraid to make decisions. She may wait for others to make a decision and then follow their choice.
- May have a poor self-concept and make negative remarks about herself. She may not feel she is as good as the other girls. She may frequently say, "I can't."
- May not have high expectations of herself, since others have not had high expectations of her. Because of her poor self-concept, she may not know when she is doing a good job and may seek frequent reinforcement or frequent direction.

Social Behavior

The child:

- May appear socially immature and naive.
- May not be adept at skills such as dressing. She may not do a thorough job of washing herself or she may fail to complete a dressing task and be unaware the task is incomplete.
- May not know when people are laughing at her or when they are laughing with her. Consequently, she may continue an inappropriate behavior if other people laugh at the behavior.
- May unknowingly allow herself to be the scapegoat of a group. She may not understand when she is helping and when she is being used by others.
- May not know what information to discuss with people and what should remain private. She may tell things to strangers that should not be repeated. Example: She may tell a stranger about a private family matter such as their income, a family problem, or an embarrassing event.
- May have difficulty understanding complex rules of games. When a game has rules that change under different circumstances, the girl may not understand the distinctions. Example: In baseball you are called "out" on a third strike except when the catcher drops the ball after the swinging third strike.
- May have difficulty developing friendships with girls her age. A lack of socialization with nondisabled girls may be the reason. Inclusion will help her to develop good social skills.

ADAPTATIONS FOR GIRLS WHO HAVE MENTAL RETARDATION

Since mental retardation affects a child's total development, the following adaptations relate to several areas of a girl's life.

Supportive Behavior

Your support and encouragement are important. While her physical development will resemble that of other girls her age, keep in mind that she may lag behind other girls her age in level of learning. This will help you to adapt meaningful activities for all the girls in the troop or group.

1. Avoid placing the girl in situations where the skills needed are beyond her level. If she does not have the necessary skills to do a project, adjust her project to a level she can achieve. For example, allow her to tell a story rather than write it. This will enable her to participate with the group.

2. Do not allow other girls to ridicule her or make fun of her work. Reinforce the other girls' behavior when they encourage her.

3. When it is necessary to select another girl to assist the girl with mental retardation, choose this helper carefully. The girl should be one who understands and appreciates individual differences. And, she should know the difference between helping with an activity and doing an activity for the girl with a disability.

4. Be sure to compliment the girl for each small task she accomplishes. She needs to hear she is doing well. This should be done quietly and without drawing attention to her.

5. When talking with the girl, emphasize what is right rather than what is wrong. If a change needs to be made in a project, be very specific as you explain what to do.

6. When a behavior is inappropriate, be firm about what is wrong. Tell her the expected behavior and demonstrate the behavior for her. Do not compare her to other girls and do not make excuses for her.

Communication

When communicating with a girl who has mental retardation, use clear and precise language. Giving specific examples will help her understand what is expected.

1. Create opportunities for verbal expression. Call on her to give information or relate any positive experiences. Select ideas and topics that are very familiar to her.

2. If the girl uses immature language while talking, do not correct the language. Restate the idea using mature language for the appropriate age level.

3. If the girl does not understand the idea being discussed, restate the idea using concrete terms. Example: If freedom is the topic, use concrete examples such as ability to vote or to live where we choose.

4. The directions for a project should be listed in steps, and each step should be numbered. This will help the girl with mental retardation to remember what has been done and what still needs to be done.

> 1. Get plant, cup, dirt.
> 2. Put dirt in cup.
> 3. Put plant in dirt.
> 4. Add water.

5. During group projects, have the girl with mental retardation contribute at her level. Be sure to accept her ideas no matter how they are stated. Restate them if necessary, making sure to give her credit for the ideas. Do not, however, accept incorrect responses or incorrect information. Correct the information without belittling the girl. Your response to this type of interaction will be a model for the other girls in the troop or group.

6. Since she may have difficulty understanding directions, the girl may need the information repeated or restated using other words.

7. Use pictures and arrows to help give directions. The order of the steps can be indicated by using an arrow to point to the next step.

8. Use very exact words when explaining the directions. Try to avoid words with more than one meaning or indefinite expressions such as "Do this" or "Do that."

9. When reviewing safety matters, use demonstration and drill as much as possible.

Presentation of Materials and Activities

When presenting materials, consider the ability of the girl to understand the material. If activities are presented at an appropriate level of understanding, the girl with mental retardation can participate in the activities of the troop or group.

1. Before starting the project, introduce any related new words by giving their concrete meanings.

2. Whenever possible, use videos or pictures to introduce new topics. This gives the girl a visual as well as an auditory image to assist in her learning.

3. Working to increase the problem-solving skills of all the girls will greatly assist the girl with mental retardation. A chart listing the steps in problem-solving will help her to determine when all the steps have been completed. Teach her to do each step by asking her the following questions:
   - What is the problem?
   - What are some choices and the consequences for each choice?
   - What is your choice?
   - Was your choice good?
   - Do you need to make another choice?

4. Work to increase her ability to transfer information. When it is time to use previously learned information, discuss with her what information she is to use and ask when and where she learned it. Then discuss how she can use that information in the new situation. The best technique is to ask questions.

5. Work to increase her ability to generalize information. When items can be grouped together, point out their similarities and differences.

6. Some girls who have mental retardation may need projects with concrete activities.

7. Projects for some girls who have mental retardation should be designed around needed adaptive or vocational skills she is working on in school. Examples:
   - Purchasing clothes.
   - Applying for a job.
   - Taking trips.
   - Caring for pets.
   - Caring for clothes.
   - Traveling in the community.

8. Relate new information and learning situations to the girl's known areas of interest. Find out what things are important to the girl. Example: If she is interested in clothing, relate a project to this idea.

9. Be aware of the skills, information, and concepts that are necessary before a new task can be learned. Example: A girl must be able to correctly measure amounts before she can complete a recipe. Be sure the girl can do the prerequisite skills before introducing projects involving new skills. If she cannot do the prerequisite skills, introduce one small skill, then guide and assist her with the additional steps. Do not complete the project for her.

10. Have any reading material recorded on an audiotape and allow the girl to listen to the tape ahead of time. This will help her understand the material as it is presented.

11. When it is necessary for material to be read, discuss the information with the girl before reading is required. This will help her to understand what is being read.

12. Use color coding on materials whenever possible. Things which are to be grouped together can be marked with the same color indicator. Packages of small colored dots, which can be purchased at an office supply store, are inexpensive and are easy to use and see.

Adaptation of Materials and Activities

Adapting troop or group activities to the level of understanding of the girl with mental retardation will help her gain the most possible from the activities.

1. Reading material may need to be revised for the girl's level of comprehension. When using written materials, present only necessary information.

2. Give the girl one or two suggested activities for self-directed, independent tasks. If the other members of the troop or group are to select and design their own project, suggest two or three ideas to the girl with mental retardation to help her in selecting a project.

3. The girl may have difficulty beginning a project because she does not know where or how to start. You may need to assist her in preparing for the project and help her with the initial steps. Review all steps for the activity using simple instructions. This may have to be repeated several times. A numbered list or chart is also helpful.

4. Use a reward system to build motivation for doing a project. Remember that the girl with mental retardation may not understand the value of the project. Therefore, rewards may be needed to stimulate her interest. Examples of rewards:
   - A check by her name.
   - A star on her work.
   - Verbal recognition of achievement.
   - Smiles and praise.
   - A pat on the back.
   - A chance to help others.

5. Develop ways, other than written, to assist her in understanding a new concept. Some examples are drawing pictures, making a scrapbook, or acting out an idea.

6. If the child is not successful at a large task, divide the task into smaller steps. Have her complete these smaller steps rather than unsuccessfully try the same large step. For example, here are small steps for setting the table:
   - Have her get the napkins.
   - Have her put a napkin at each place.
   - Have her collect the correct silverware.
   - Have her put a setting at each place.
   - Have her gather the different-sized plates.
   - Have her put these plates in their appropriate places.
   - Have her get out the appropriate glasses.
   - Have her put the glasses in place.

7. Since it may take the girl additional attempts to learn new information, provide a time during the meeting to review any new information or to practice a new skill. Without drawing attention to the girl, assist her in going over the information or practicing the skill.

Memory and Organization

1. Provide an outline of the important points in a reading selection. This will help her identify and remember what is important and what is minor detail.

2. Have her make notes and help her develop a calendar to assist in remembering future events and responsibilities.

3. Reduce possible distractions in the work environment. Reducing noise by closing doors and sitting away from windows will help the girl concentrate on the project work.

4. Be very exact in stating what is expected. If you want the girl to put items in a certain order, be sure to state the order. Do not assume the girl will know you want large items first then small items, or green items first then all blue items.

Behavior

1. Work to increase the girl's self-awareness. Speak to her frequently about her talents. However, do not tell her she is good at something she does not do well. Also, ask her to tell you what she can do well and what she needs to work on improving. Support and encourage her as she attempts new tasks regardless of how simple the task.

2. Work to increase her self-confidence. Have her do activities that are confidence-building. Have her tell the group something about herself. Have her deliver messages. Let her suggest troop or group activities. Openly speak of her contribution to the troop or group.

3. When her emotional response is immature, do not make fun of the response. Accept the feeling and suggest a more mature response. Example: "It is good to feel happy. Next time why don't you clap your hands like this." It is a good idea to model the suggested response.

FAMOUS PEOPLE

While many people with mental retardation have accomplished a great deal and have made significant contributions to society, they have not often been recognized. Some of these people are mentioned here. Look around your own community, and contact local organizations for names of famous people with mental retardation.

Chris Burke, *actor*
Rosemary Kennedy, *inspiration for Special Olympics*

Chapter 7

Behavior Disorders

In the course of a day, a week, or a month we experience many different feelings such as happiness, sadness, anger, love, fear, and excitement. When we experience a feeling, we respond with a behavior. For most people their behavioral response to the feeling or emotion is not considered unusual. However, for others, the feeling is so intense that the behavioral response is not only noticed by others, but appears inappropriate. When this happens too frequently, and over too long a period of time, the person may be considered to have a behavior problem or a behavior disorder.

Probably more than any other group of people with disabilities, people with behavior disorders are the most misunderstood. The complexity of this disability is indicated in the confusion among the experts over the definitions and the many names used to identify the disability. Some commonly used terms are behavior disorders, behavior disturbances, behavior problems, emotional disorders, emotional disturbances, or emotional maladjustment. Girls with attention deficit disorders (ADD), learning disabilities, autism, or those facing temporary crises, may also have problems managing behavior. To avoid confusion, the single term "behavior disorder" will be used throughout this chapter.

The factors that are used in most definitions and that apply to all of the aforementioned terms are:

1. The child displays behaviors not in the range of behaviors considered typical for children of the same age and sex.
2. The behaviors occur too frequently and too intensely.
3. The behaviors occur and recur over an extended period of time.

52

All behaviors are on a continuum. When the behavior displayed is at either end of the continuum, the behavior is not considered typical.

EXAMPLE: AMOUNT OF TALKING

Never talks	Talks only if required	Participates in conversations both serious and social	Talks at every opportunity	Consistently interrupts others

The behavior of a girl who never talks or one who consistently interrupts others to talk is not appropriate. If either of these talking behaviors happens frequently during many consecutive meetings, the behavior meets the criteria of a behavior disorder.

Sometimes a behavior at the far end of a continuum will happen only a few times or for a short duration. All girls experience emotional upsets over such occurrences as a quarrel with a friend or the death of a pet. However, the distressed behavior will usually be of short duration and will lessen over time. As the leader, you need to let the girl know you care about her feelings, whether the upset is of long or short duration, while acknowledging that her feelings are legitimate. Situations that are trivial to an adult may be very real and important to children and youths.

Because of varying life events, one person may have a behavior disorder at only one period in her life while others may have problems for years. Advances in therapy and treatment can help a person eliminate a behavior disorder, either by dealing with the problem directly or by learning appropriate ways to express her behavioral response to a feeling. This disability can be treated through timely and appropriate intervention.

Even though a behavior disorder condition is difficult to define, we know that children do have behavior disorders which need adult support. These children have inner stress that creates emotional pain or actions that are beyond their control. Working with children who exhibit behavior disorders can be frustrating because we often can do little to solve their problem or lessen the pain. What we, as adults in the girl's life, can do is provide a stable and trusting environment for her, even if it is only for one or two hours a week.

Approximately 9 percent of the school-age children in our society qualify through their public and private schools for special assistance as children with behavior disorders or emotional disturbance (see table on page 5). Bear in mind that children with behavior disorders are a cross-section of the population. The learning abilities of these children range from delayed in development to very bright, and they come from a wide range of family backgrounds. It is the intensity, frequency, and duration of the behavioral response that indicate a girl is dealing with inner stress.

While the behavior of the child with a behavior disorder is unpredictable and can be disruptive, keep in mind that this girl is not really directing the behavior at you or at any other person during the meeting or outing. She is responding to her inner stress or pain. Remembering this may help you to respond in a calm and caring manner.

MYTHS AND STEREOTYPES

Many myths and stereotypes are associated with behavior disorders. These untrue and generalized ideas interfere with our understanding of the disability. Lack of accurate information hinders our ability to fully appreciate the contributions that people with behavior disorders can make to society. Some common misconceptions about people with a behavior disorder are that they:

- Could get over the problem if they just tried.
- Inherited the problem.
- Act that way to get attention.
- Are dangerous and cannot be trusted.
- Are that way because their parents are poor disciplinarians.
- Are crazy.

It is important to work to eliminate any myths or stereotypical beliefs expressed by the other members of the troop or group.

CHARACTERISTICS

The primary difference between a girl with a behavior disorder and other girls her age is the manner in which she responds to her feelings. Some characteristics of children with behavior problems are listed below. As with all of the disabilities being discussed, remember that the girl is more like other girls her own age than she is different. A child with a behavior disorder may exhibit just a few or she may exhibit several of these characteristics.

Motor Behavior

The child:

- May seem to be in constant motion. The amount of motion shown is inappropriate for her age or for the current activity.
- May move aimlessly around the room and may appear to have no purpose as she does so.

Learning Ability

The child:

- May have difficulty concentrating.
- May work hastily and carelessly. At times, it may appear she is not interested in the activity. Remember, she may be interested in the work but may be afraid of failing, due to earlier failures.
- May seem easily distracted. Noises and sights that do not seem to bother the other girls may distract her.
- May be impulsive. She may act without thought and deliberation. She may shout out an answer before the question is fully read.
- May frequently use attention-seeking behaviors. She may repeatedly ask for your help or she may correct what other girls say or do.
- May experience school failure. Her academic progress may be behind that of peers and below her ability level.

Communication Ability

The child:

- May make verbal outbursts. She may interrupt you or the other troop or group members; she may make irrelevant comments, argue with the other girls, or disrupt the order and flow of the meeting.
- May make inappropriate noises. Example: She may make animal noises or clicking noises with her mouth.
- May avoid eye contact. When you talk to her, she may look in another direction.
- May refuse to talk to you or to the other members of the troop or group.

Emotional Behavior

The child:

- May exhibit a general mood of unhappiness.
- May make negative remarks about herself.
- May be anxious over events that are neither new nor difficult. She may strive for perfection and show an inability to relax.
- May isolate herself from other Girl Scouts. She may sit alone when going on a trip or she may sit off by herself at a meeting.
- May threaten to injure herself or others.
- May seem hostile. Her reaction to the leaders and the other group members may show suspicion, hostility, and anger.

- May be dependent on you, the leader, or on another Girl Scout when decisions and choices must be made. There may be excessive clinging, fearfulness, and need for frequent reassurance.
- May cry unexpectedly. She may burst into tears for no apparent reason. Remember that the tears are a response to her inner stress. Just because the reason is not evident to you does not mean the reason is not real to her.

Social Behavior

The child:

- May have a difficult time making friends. Her behavior could be either too aggressive or too withdrawn.
- May have a difficult time maintaining friendships for an extended period of time.
- May have a difficult time following rules set by authorities.
- May verbally or physically assault others.
- May have inappropriate affective behaviors. She may laugh at people's misfortune, or express happiness when others are hurt.
- May blame others for her mistakes.
- May engage in socially unacceptable behavior, such as lying or stealing.
- May talk about unacceptable things—for example, sexual parts or acts, parents' personal life, body elimination.
- May use inappropriate language—for example, swearing to get attention.

ADAPTATIONS FOR GIRLS WITH BEHAVIOR DISORDERS

The adaptations for children with a behavior disorder have two objectives. The first is to provide a warm and accepting environment; the second is to maintain a structured environment where expectations are clear.

Many of the adaptations in the chapter on learning disabilities are also appropriate for girls with a behavior disorder. These strategies

may also be helpful for any girl with disruptive behavior, whether or not she has a disability.

Supportive Behavior

Since the girl feels a great amount of inner stress, try to be supportive and create an environment that does not increase her stress. Following are some suggestions to assist you in establishing a warm and stable environment.

1. Set fair and firm limits. Do not set limits that cannot be met.
2. Involve all of the girls in setting the rules or policies for the troop or group.
3. Be consistent. Meetings and meeting environments should have structure and predictability from week to week. This is important for any girl, but is particularly critical for the girl with a behavior disorder. If you say a certain event will happen, see that the event does happen. If the event does not take place, calmly explain the reason for the changes. Be prompt and honest with your explanations for the girl with a behavior disorder and for the entire group.
4. Be consistent with other helping adults in the girl's life—her teacher, counselor, and parents. Find out what help she is receiving and what her ground rules and rewards are.

5. Provide frequent and positive attention. Do not wait for a disruption to occur before speaking to the girl with a behavior disorder. Let her know you noticed the appropriate things she does.

6. Provide a time-out space for inappropriate or cooling-down behavior for all girls in the troop or group. This should be a place where you mutually agree the child needs to go for a specific period of time. Ask the girl if she needs some time to herself before she returns to the group, and indicate the time-out place. This then becomes a strategy rather than a punishment.

7. Pay close attention to the intonation used by the child with a behavior disorder. This may help you to identify the emotional stress the girl is experiencing. A sharp statement or a "yes" or "no" through clenched teeth indicates more than the other words she is saying.

8. Since a girl with a behavior disorder is usually not aware of her own progress, it is a good idea to indicate her progress directly and specifically to her. For example, you might point to her project and say, "Last week you got four _____ finished and this week you finished six _____." This could be anything from the number of stitches in a sewing project to the number of seeds planted. Another suggestion is to indicate her progress visually by marking what she has achieved on a chart.

9. Remind the girl ahead of time when projects are due.

10. Alert the group ahead of time when a new activity is about to take place.

11. Include the child in group and troop projects by pairing her with a girl the same age. Select the partner carefully. She should be outgoing but not overpowering or dominating.

12. Notice whether she is paying attention. If not, stand closer to her to encourage her to pay attention.

Communication

Communication between you and the girl can influence the amount of stress she feels. Effective communication is crucial in establishing a trusting environment.

Here are some ideas for clear communication.

1. Use very precise language. The child with a behavior disorder will need to know exactly what behaviors are expected of her.

2. Keep your voice at an even pitch. Raising the pitch of your voice may add to the girl's emotional tension and result in inappropriate behavior.

3. Do not use sarcasm. This could cause additional inner pain and result in an emotional reaction.

4. Encourage the child to think before she speaks. Have the entire group observe a five- or ten-second "think time" before answering a question or responding to a situation.

5. Do not begin giving directions until the child is paying attention.

6. Give directions for a project in a clear and concise manner; state only essential information. It is a good idea to number each step of the directions.

7. Before presenting important oral information, give a signal to alert the girl with a behavior disorder that something important is to follow. Be sure to use this cue only when necessary during the meeting or outing. Example: "Ready? Listen."

8. When she does not follow directions, find out whether she fully understands what is expected. She may understand only part of the directions and may be guessing at the rest. If she does understand the directions, return her attention to the project in an uncritical manner.

9. The child with a behavior disorder will need frequent and specific feedback. Such feedback tells the girl exactly what she has done well or what needs to be improved. For example, general feedback would be, "Good report." Specific feedback would be, "You did a good job sharing your experience about going to the zoo. You kept your eyes on the audience and your information was interesting."

Presentation of Materials and Activities

A clear and precise presentation of materials and activities helps the girl with a behavior disorder understand what is expected.

1. Help girls to predict activities, and thus better manage their own behavior. Girl planning, kaper charts, posted meeting agendas, and calendars of activities are all helpful and give girls a sense of control over their environment.

2. Be sure you make eye contact with the girl before beginning a presentation.

3. Start off the meeting with activities that the girl with a behavior disorder likes and in which she does well. This will start the meeting on a positive note.

4. Help the child budget her time by dividing the meeting into sections. Let her know what should be completed during each time period. It is often useful to post a list of the activities being done. Give positive verbal support when the girl completes the designated tasks.

5. Make a list of materials needed to complete a project. Have the girl assemble these materials prior to beginning work.

6. When the girl must make a choice, be very specific on what choices are available. It may be a good idea to limit the number of choices. Example: "You may have either an apple or an orange."

Adaptation of Materials and Activities

The abilities of the girl with a behavior disorder will be similar to those of all girls her age. The main idea behind adapting the materials and activities is to increase the girl's feeling of success and instill positive feelings about herself.

1. Provide the girl with an example of the outcome of a project. This gives her a specific goal to work toward.

2. Carefully design projects and activities for successful completion. The first steps of all projects should be the easiest steps. This encourages the girl to continue and to have a successful experience with the project.

3. Present work in small segments. When one segment is complete, give her the second segment. Be sure to praise her as she completes each segment.

4. The child may need more frequent reinforcement for showing appropriate behaviors than may the other members of the troop or group. Try to use reinforcements that are social and not tangible. Some suggestions for social reinforcers are:
   - Being leader of an event.
   - Demonstrating a skill before the troop.
   - Being asked to run errands.
   - Having her projects displayed.
   - Receiving verbal praise.
   - Being patted on the shoulder.
   - Receiving direct and frequent smiles.

Memory and Organizational Skills

Because of the inner stress, a girl with a behavior disorder may have a difficult time remembering, or may have a great deal of difficulty organizing her projects and activities. Here are some strategies that you can try to assist her:

1. Have the entire group make a list of things to bring to the next meeting. This list will help the girl with the behavior disorder.
2. When all is going well, remind the child of things to remember. She may have more difficulty remembering when under stress.
3. Provide the girl with an individual work space where there are few distractions. Do not, however, isolate her from the group.
4. Help her to organize her materials. Divide a notebook into sections to help the girl locate specific items when called upon to do so.

Behavior

The girl with a behavior disorder will gain self-confidence as she learns appropriate social interaction skills.

1. Permit unstructured time or time for physical activity. There should be times when the girl with a behavior disorder is allowed to move around the meeting room or go on errands for the leader.
2. The girl with a behavior disorder may need written contracts (see sample above). In setting up a contract, keep these points in mind:
   - The written agreement should be positive. Avoid using negative statements.
   - The leader should not determine all parts of the written agreement; it must be a joint decision.
   - The appropriate behavior should come before the reward.
   - The reward should immediately follow the performance of the appropriate behavior.
   - Be sure to let the girl help determine the reward. Just because you like something or feel it is an appropriate reward does not mean it will be pleasing to her.

CONTRACT FOR ALICIA

Action	Achievement	Reward
I will raise my hand before speaking.	(Five tries in a row without reminders.)	
I will respect others' property.	(Five times in a row asking to borrow before taking.)	
	Give a compliment instead of damaging someone else's things. (Five times in a row show success.)	

Sample Contract

3. Set very specific consequences for any inappropriate behavior. These consequences should apply to all of the troop or group members, and you should always follow through with the established consequences. Determining consequences before the behavior occurs will eliminate much of the criticizing and blaming that can follow inappropriate behavior.
4. Give her some examples of non-aggressive behaviors that she can use in a situation which could become aggressive. Example: Telling another girl when something has happened instead of reacting. She could say, "You stepped on my toe," rather than hitting the girl.
5. Use role-playing to help the girl practice appropriate group behaviors and appropriate responses to emotional situations.
6. When she responds in an appropriate way, be sure to acknowledge her correct behavior. Your recognition may prompt other appropriate behaviors.
7. For the girl who exhibits withdrawal, identify her strengths and weaknesses. Encourage her to participate in activities in which she has strong abilities.

8. Reinforce appropriate behaviors for all the Girl Scouts, such as waiting their turn to speak. This will take the focus away from inappropriate behavior, and provide a good model for appropriate ways to gain attention.

9. If the girl becomes upset, remain calm but firm. If she is disturbing others, remove her from the setting until she is calm. Be sure an adult remains with her. Do not discuss the appropriate behavior until the situation has calmed. Discussion while the girl is upset will only add more tension to an already stressful situation.

10. Be willing to listen to the girl if she seems to need to discuss something. Do not try to solve her problem, however. Her need is to know that she can talk to you in confidence. Do not repeat any information she tells you unless it is life-threatening or illegal. In such a case, tell her you will have to share this information with _____ (name or title of the person).

11. Pay close attention to her nonverbal behavior. You may be able to prevent disruptive behavior if you notice tense muscles, a strained look around the eyes, or clenched fists. When you notice these symptoms of tension, try to eliminate the tension that the girl is experiencing without lessening group standards. You might let her take time away from her project to work on a relaxing activity or ask her to run an errand.

12. Do not be afraid to identify the feeling the girl is indicating through her behavior. When the child with a behavior disorder appears to be feeling anger, for example, you might say, "You seem to be feeling angry about this. It is all right to feel angry but I cannot let you (name the disruptive behavior)." As the leader, you are telling the child that you accept her feelings, but you do not accept the way she is responding to those feelings. You may need to give her an alternative way to respond. Example: Tell the girl, "When you feel angry, it is okay to look out the window or read a book." Be sure to emphasize the appropriate behavior rather than criticizing the feeling. Often you will need to repeat this in many situations before the girl will feel comfortable or will trust you.

13. When a girl with a behavior disorder makes a negative statement about herself, respond with a positive opinion about her. However, do not argue with her about her abilities. Example:

Girl Scout: "I can't do anything right."

Leader: "I think you do a nice job with many things. You are very good at (name some specific skill she does well)."

Girl Scout: "No, I'm not."

Leader: "I gave you my opinion and I will not change it." Repeat the statements, "I think you do a nice job with many things. You are very good at..." (repeat the same behavior mentioned the first time you made the statement). Do not continue further; change the subject. Arguing only reinforces her negative behavior. Moving on will force her to think about something else.

14. Treat any threat to do harm to herself as real. Discuss any remarks of this type with her parents or guardian.

15. It may be helpful to read some of the GSUSA books in the "Issues for Girl Scouts" series. This information can add to your understanding of children with behavior problems.

FAMOUS PEOPLE

Many people with behavior disorders can and do lead successful lives. Listed below are some successful people who have or had a behavior disorder at one time in their lives.

Joan Crawford, *actress*
Patty Duke, *actress*
Thomas Eagleton, *politician*
Connie Francis, *singer*
Vladimir Horowitz, *musician*
Margot Kidder, *actress*
Vivien Leigh, *actress*
Mary Todd Lincoln, *wife of Abraham Lincoln*
Jim Piersall, *baseball player*
Robert Schumann, *composer*

Chapter 8

Hearing Impairments

Hearing is an important means of learning from the time a child is born. An infant not only learns to recognize environmental sounds and the sounds of voices, but also learns to speak and to develop language skills through hearing the sound of her own voice and hearing other people use language. These skills in turn are critical in developing social and cultural ties.

If the ability to hear is impaired, the development of speech and language is delayed. This places a great limitation on the child with a hearing impairment in developing the needed communication skills and social skills that are dependent on speech and language. The girl with a hearing loss must depend on other senses, such as sight, to learn language and social skills.

FACTORS TO CONSIDER IN ADAPTING ACTIVITIES

Sounds are measured by their loudness (decibel level) and pitch (hertz). Two factors will help the leader determine necessary adaptation of activities for a Girl Scout with a hearing loss–the type of loss and its severity.

Type of Hearing Loss

CONDUCTIVE HEARING LOSS

A conductive hearing loss is the result of obstructions or diseases of the outer or middle ear. All sounds from the highest to the lowest decibel level may be affected, but the loss is seldom severe. The girl with this type of hearing loss will generally benefit from using a hearing aid, surgery, or both.

SENSORINEURAL LOSS

This type of hearing loss occurs following damage to the hair cells of the inner ear or the nerves leading to it. The hearing loss may range from mild to profound (see below), and may only affect certain pitches. Thus, a hearing aid does little to improve this type of loss, since sounds may still be too distorted to be understood.

MIXED LOSS

A mixed loss is a combination of a conductive and sensorineural loss, and means problems in the outer and either middle or inner ear.

CENTRAL LOSS

When there is damage to the nerves of the central nervous system, either in the brain or the channels leading to it, a central hearing loss results. Like the sensorineural loss, this is seldom helped with hearing aids.

Severity of Hearing Loss

MILD

A girl with a mild hearing loss will have difficulty hearing whispers, soft sounds, distant sounds, or speech. She may not realize she has a hearing loss.

MODERATE

A girl with a moderate hearing loss will have difficulty understanding a conversation unless it is within three to five feet. She will also miss some detail in group discussion.

SEVERE

This girl will not be able to hear any loud sounds occurring beyond a distance of one to two feet. She may not be able to distinguish environmental sounds.

PROFOUND

This girl will probably not rely on hearing as a primary source of learning. Other senses will need to be used to gain information from the environment.

Additional Terminology

Other terms commonly used to identify an individual's hearing loss are "deaf" and "hard of hearing."

"Deaf" is used to describe a hearing loss which is so severe that the person is impaired in understanding oral language with or without amplification, and educational performance is adversely affected. This term is used when the hearing loss falls in the severe or profound range, 90 decibels or higher.

"Hard of hearing" is used to describe a hearing impairment, whether permanent or fluctuating, which adversely affects a child's educational performance but which is not under the definition of deaf. This term is used when the hearing loss falls in the mild or moderate range.

Caution must be exercised when using any classification system because girls with identical hearing losses may function differently. Each girl must be viewed as an individual with unique learning characteristics.

MYTHS AND STEREOTYPES

As with all disabilities, there are untrue beliefs or myths associated with a hearing impairment. These myths, which have developed over many years, limit expectations of people with a hearing loss. People tend to apply stereotypes to all people with a hearing loss when, in fact, the stereotypical characteristics do not apply. This tendency leads to misinformation and a poor understanding of individuals with a hearing loss.

Some common myths and stereotypes are listed below.

People with a hearing loss:

- Are dumb.
- Hear what they want to hear.
- Are cranky.
- Would rather be with other people with a hearing loss.
- All use sign language.

CHARACTERISTICS

Motor Behavior

The child:

- May turn or tilt her head to one side when listening. She may need to position one ear toward the speaker to hear adequately.
- May have a problem with equilibrium. She may lose her balance when walking or making sudden turns.

Learning Ability

The child:

- May appear to be inattentive when people are speaking. Either she cannot hear the sounds, or the sounds are so distorted that she has difficulty understanding and concentrating on what is being said.
- May have difficulty following oral instructions and may get directions confused. She may not have heard the information or may not have heard enough of the information to know what is expected.

Communication Ability

The child:

- May use immature, unusual, or distorted speech. We learn to speak by repeating what we hear. Since the Girl Scout with a hearing loss may not hear sounds accurately, her speech may be distorted.
- May have difficulty understanding abstract concepts and ideas.
- May be reluctant to participate in oral activities such as group discussions.
- May have difficulty understanding words that have more than one meaning. *Examples:*
  - Please open the can.
  - I can go fast.
  - He can run fast.
  - There is a run in my stocking.
- May often fail to grasp the point of a joke or riddle. Her language skills may not be adequate to understand the answer or punch line.
- May speak very quietly or very loudly, depending on the degree of hearing loss.
- May speak in a monotone. Some girls with a hearing loss will not change their tone of voice to add meaning and emphasis to a sentence.
- May not understand communication of meaning through change in voice tone. If you use intonation or raise your voice to indicate questions, she may not know you are asking a question and may not give you an answer.
- May confuse words that have similar sounds. Words such as "feel" and "fill" or "chose" and "shows" may be misunderstood. The sentence, "She chose the blue dress" could be heard as "She shows the blue dress."
- May use one of three means of communication:

MANUAL

There are several forms of manual communication or sign language. The most commonly used form is American Sign Language (ASL), which is the third most

used language in the United States. This language uses both finger spelling and signs for words or ideas. ASL has its own set of rules for the formation of signs and is not an exact manual form of English. Some girls may use another manual language, signed English, in school, but may use ASL or some other method of communication in social settings. If the girl uses a manual method of communication, an auxiliary form of communication, such as an interpreter, may be needed.

ORAL-AURAL

This form of communication stresses the use of the residual or remaining hearing combined with speech reading. A girl using this means of communication will depend on watching the speaker's face and other forms of visual information. In her own communications she will use speech.

TOTAL COMMUNICATION

Total communication combines the manual and the oral-aural methods. The girl will be skilled at speech reading and oral communication as well as signing and finger spelling.

Emotional Behavior

The child:

- May seem stubborn. She may not have heard part of the information and therefore does not know you gave the information.
- May be shy or withdrawn. Because the girl with a hearing loss may miss all or parts of conversations, she may feel isolated. This feeling may lead to withdrawal from the group.
- May feel people are talking about her. She may see girls talking in small groups and not hear what they are saying. As a result, she may assume they are talking about her.
- May have a poor self-concept and may make negative statements about herself.

Social Behavior

The child:

- May act out, try to call attention to herself in inappropriate ways, or leave the group because she feels left out or does not understand what is going on.
- May prefer to work in small groups. The conversation of a few people talking is easier to follow than many people holding a conversation.
- May develop a dependence on her peers for needed instruction. She may wait until others begin their work before starting her own project. She may rely on watching the group to find out when to start or what to do.
- May not know current slang terms. This can hinder social interaction with girls her own age.
- May have a difficult time knowing the meaning of idioms and figures of speech. Example: "I am dog tired." This idiom could be interpreted as "The dogs are tired" or "I am a tired dog."

Sensory Characteristics

The Girl Scout with a hearing loss may have fluctuations in her ability to hear. She may be able to hear better on some days than on other days.

As the troop or group leader, you may observe undiagnosed hearing problems. Some signs are:

- Draining ears.
- Continuous mouth breathing.
- Constant pulling or tugging at her ears.
- Seems more aware of movement or actions than of sound.
- Does not seem to understand oral directions.
- Appears inattentive, bored, or fidgety during group discussion.
- Asks for information to be repeated.

ADAPTATIONS FOR GIRLS WITH HEARING IMPAIRMENTS

Adaptations for a Girl Scout with a hearing loss are focused on adjusting the method of presenting information and of directing activities. With a hearing loss, the child will often have to use her other senses to obtain information and to communicate with others.

Supportive Behavior

A Girl Scout with a hearing loss may miss important parts of communication. It is important that you, the leader, be supportive of her and her efforts to participate in activities.

1. View the hearing loss as only one characteristic and not the most important characteristic of the individual girl.
2. For the girl who uses a hearing aid, remember that the hearing aid cannot replace the natural hearing function of the ear. Any Girl Scout who wears a hearing aid does not hear the same way with the aid that hearing persons do. If you have a troop or group member who wears a hearing aid, remember the following:
   - Speak in a normal tone.
   - Face the girl. She may need to speech-read.
   - Keep in mind that a hearing aid does not make speech sound the same as what you hear.
   - During water activities you may have to remind the girl to remove her hearing aid so it does not get wet.
   - When the girl who regularly participates in discussion does not participate, make sure the hearing aid battery is not dead.
   - If you are going on an overnight trip, you might have the girl bring an extra battery.
   - If the Girl Scout repeatedly removes the aid, this may indicate the aid is not working properly. It would be a good idea to mention this to her family.
3. A Girl Scout with a hearing loss may tire more easily than other girls. Watching people's faces for an extended period of time can be very tiring. If needed, allow the child with a hearing loss to take rest periods from speech reading. You might give both oral and written directions before project work.
4. Call attention to the visible aspects of any ideas or activities. Example: If the troop or group is working on a service project at the library, point out the things they will see at the library and the resources available.
5. Encourage the Girl Scout with a hearing loss to ask questions if she is not sure of what has been said. Remember, it may take two or three questions for her to fully understand the information. Do not be impatient when answering questions. Treat each question as an important part of the total picture.
6. When you respond to a question from a child with a hearing loss, try not to draw attention to her. Do not give rambling answers. Respond with brief, condensed answers in a quiet tone of voice.
7. If the child with a hearing loss becomes frustrated when she does not understand something, rephrase the statements. Do not repeat using the same words.
8. Use a visual signal to gather troop or group members when out-of-doors, such as a flashing light.
9. The Girl Scouts in the troop or group may wish to learn the form of sign language used by a girl in their troop or group who has a hearing impairment. If a girl uses a manual system, contact your local agency for people with hearing impairments to secure a speaker who can provide instruction to the troop or group. It is important to locate a qualified instructor for sign language instruction. There are no home-training programs.
10. Do not call attention to the speech errors of a girl with a hearing loss.
11. If the girl has better hearing in one ear, position yourself so that she hears you from her better ear.

12. The Girl Scout with a hearing loss may need a buddy to help with directions when you are not available. Be sure to select the buddy carefully, or let the Girl Scout with the hearing loss select her own buddy. The buddy should be a girl who is sensitive to both the girl's need for assistance and her need for independence.

Communication

1. When talking to a child with a hearing loss, speak in a normal tone of voice and with normal rhythm. There is no need to shout or to speak slowly. The girl who is speech reading will be confused by exaggerated mouth movements.
2. During a group discussion, have the other girls turn to face the Girl Scout with a hearing loss when they speak.
3. Use good speech patterns. Be clear in your pronunciation of words.
4. Having something in your mouth makes speech reading difficult; avoid chewing movements as much as possible. Face toward the girl when speaking and remember to enunciate clearly.
5. Make your comments to her clear and to the point, free from extraneous information.
6. If you have difficulty understanding the child, ask her to repeat what she said. If you still have difficulty understanding, ask her to write it down or to show you. Let her know that what she has to say is important.
7. When going on field trips or attending other events, ask ahead of time if special equipment or interpreters are available for girls who will need them.
8. When giving directions, face the group or troop.
9. Stand in one place while giving directions.
10. In addition to giving directions orally, also write them on a chalkboard or on a poster. Number the steps of the directions as you give them.

11. Use full sentences when speaking rather than one-word directions. When directions are not understood, repeat or rephrase the entire sentence.

Presentation of Materials and Activities

The following suggestions will help you in making clear presentations to the girl with a hearing loss.

1. Allow the Girl Scout to pre-read any information that will be given orally.
2. Avoid standing in dark areas while speaking. Also avoid standing in front of windows because your face will be in a shadow. Speech reading is difficult when there is insufficient light on the speaker's face.
3. Be careful that you do not turn your back when speaking to the group. The Girl Scout with a hearing loss will not be able to see your mouth to speech read.
4. When speaking, be careful that you do not turn your head or place your hand next to or over your mouth. The girl with a hearing loss cannot see your mouth properly to speech read if you turn away or cover your mouth.

5. Have the troop or group decide on visual techniques for you to gain their attention. Turning the lights off and on is one good method. The Girl Scout signal of raising the hand is also a good technique.

6. Use as much written or illustrated material as possible. By providing visual material, you encourage the child with a hearing loss to participate in all possible activities.

7. When referring to an object in the room, go to the object and touch it. When referring to an object during a discussion, use the name of the object rather than "this" or "that."

8. When you are talking about a model or an example, touch or point to the specific part as it is being discussed.

Adaptation of Materials and Activities

The following suggestions will help in adapting materials and activities for the Girl Scout with a hearing loss.

1. When the troop or group will be answering questions or discussing a topic, put this information on a chart so the girl with a hearing loss will understand the information and will be able to participate.

2. If notes are to be taken—for example, when you have a meeting guest or take a trip—have another Girl Scout make a photocopy of the notes. Remember, the Girl Scout with a hearing loss cannot take notes and speech read at the same time.

3. Because the Girl Scout with a hearing loss may not be reading at her age level, she may need extra time to comprehend written material presented during a meeting. As noted earlier, it may be advisable to let her review a copy of printed materials ahead of time.

4. During a presentation, use a visual signal when it is time for group discussion to begin. Before a girl starts to speak, she could raise a finger, raise her hand, or nod her head. This gives the Girl Scout with the hearing loss the time to locate the speaker.

Memory and Organization

1. Give the Girl Scout with a hearing loss a written list of the steps in each task or the specific items to be brought to the next meeting.

2. Provide the troop or group with a written reminder of important dates. A calendar with notes on the appropriate dates will help the girl with a hearing loss.

WORK SPACE

The following suggestions can help you develop a work space that is most comfortable for the Girl Scout with a hearing loss.

1. Encourage the Girl Scout with a hearing loss to select seating where she can make the best use of her ability to hear.

2. The Girl Scout with a hearing loss should sit so she can see as many faces as possible. This includes the leaders as well as the other girls.

3. Seating should be arranged so that the child with a hearing loss does not look directly into a light or at a window.

4. Keep background noise to a minimum. For some girls with a hearing loss, many different sounds at the same time can be very distracting. Close a door or window to help lessen noise. The Girl Scout with a hearing loss should not sit next to the source of any background noise, such as a motor or a fan.

5. When playing music, put a speaker on a wooden floor or put a CD or cassette player on a table so the girl with a hearing loss can feel the vibrations.

BEHAVIOR

1. The same behavior standards should be used for all the Girl Scouts in the troop or group. If you have two sets of expected behavior, the girls may resent the differing standards.

2. At times, a girl with a hearing loss may feel isolated from the group. The other members of the troop or group need to learn how to recognize when the girl with a hearing impairment is feeling this way and should develop natural ways to include her in social groups. *Example:* Girls can approach the Girl Scout with a hearing loss rather than asking her to come to the group.

Also, have the other Girl Scouts ask the girl with a hearing loss for her opinions, ideas, or help.

FAMOUS PEOPLE

People with a hearing impairment can be successful in all fields of work. Listed below are some examples. You may want to add some from your community.

Stephanie Beacham, *actress*
Ludwig van Beethoven, *composer*
Alexander Graham Bell, *inventor*
Linda Bove, *actress*
Amelia Earhart, *aviator*
Nanette Fabray, *actress*
Phyllis Frelich, *actress*
Helen Keller, *author, lecturer*
Juliette Gordon Low, *founder of Girl Scouts of the U.S.A.*
Marlee Matlin, *actress*
Kitty O'Neill, *stuntwoman*
Ronald Reagan, *U.S. President*
Heather Whitestone, *first deaf Miss America, dancer, speaker*

Chapter 9

Visual Impairments

Among people with visual impairments, there is a large difference in their ability to see. No two people with a visual impairment are alike and each should be treated as an individual.

Few people have a visual problem that cannot be corrected with glasses. Only 1 percent of the total population is classified as visually impaired. These people have a severe vision problem that is not correctable with glasses: they may need adjustments in the physical environment, in the method of instruction, and in the materials they use. It is important for you, the Girl Scout leader, to be aware of their individual needs so you can make needed adaptations. People with a visual impairment do not necessarily have other senses that are better, but must learn to use their senses of hearing, touch, smell, and taste to supplement visual messages received from other people. They must compensate to live and function in a sighted world.

CLASSIFICATIONS

A visual impairment is the result of a functional loss of vision, rather than a disorder of the eye itself. The selection of appropriate activities depends on the degree of loss, when the loss of vision occurred, and the kind of loss.

Degree of Loss

Partially sighted indicates that the girl has corrected (with glasses) vision lower than the average sighted person, but significant vision remains. She will need some adaptations both at school and in the community.

Low vision means a significant loss of sight, and not necessarily just with distance vision. A person with low vision would be unable to read the newspaper at a typical distance, even with glasses. A girl with this condition may need adaptations in lighting, may need to read large print (sometimes Braille), and will rely on her other senses to learn.

Legally blind refers to someone whose corrected vision is 20/200 or less, or who has a narrow field of vision.

Totally blind indicates a degree of loss so severe that the girl will not be able to learn through any visual means. Very few people are totally blind.

Girls with the same degree of vision loss will probably not be able to see at the same level. Some girls will be able to use more of their remaining vision than will other girls. This means that girls with the same degree of visual loss will have different learning needs. Other factors may also affect learning, as discussed below.

When Loss of Vision Occurred

If the loss happened before birth or very early in life, learning can be more difficult. The difficulty is not because of inability to learn but because the person does not have visual images for reference. If you say, "See the pretty blue mountains next to the green field," the girl who lost significant vision early in life would have no previously learned information to use as a basis to form this mental picture. The girl who lost her vision later in life can form a picture of what is being discussed because she has seen color, mountains, and fields.

Kind of Loss

In addition to the degree of loss or when the loss occurred, the kind of loss will affect the types of adaptations girls may need.

CENTRAL VISION LOSS

This girl cannot see what is directly in front of her. She can only see what is at the edge of her field of vision. She will turn her head to an angle and will appear to be looking at something else when in fact she is looking at you.

TUNNEL VISION

This girl can only see what is directly in front of her. Her vision appears as if she is looking through a long tube. She will have to move her head from side to side to see the total picture. Because she sees only part of an image at a time, she will receive information in bits and pieces.

CLOUDY VISION

Images will appear as through a fog. This girl will not see detail and will have difficulty seeing objects or people in the distance. She may have difficulty anticipating approaching objects such as traffic or a ball.

DISTORTED OR BLURRED VISION

Images will appear fuzzy and blurred. This girl will have difficulty identifying detail, and reading will be difficult.

Not only do the above factors affect the learning needs of the girl but other factors, including the girl's personal history, are also an influence. All factors combine to create the individual and determine her abilities and limitations.

It is helpful to view girls' abilities as falling on a continuum. That is, a girl may have any degree of a characteristic, ranging from minimum ability to maximum ability.

EXAMPLE: READING PRINT				
Cannot see print	Can read newspaper headlines	Can read large print	Can read most print	Can read fine detail

←—————————————————→

Girls who have difficulty reading print may excel in many other activities. When you view each characteristic on a continuum, you will find the Girl Scout with a visual impairment more like girls her age than different.

MYTHS AND STEREOTYPES

Some of the oldest myths and stereotypes are related to visual impairments. A common untrue belief is that people with visual impairments have better hearing than other people. Myth: The person with a visual impairment always knows her location based on the sounds around her.

What people misunderstand is that a person with a visual impairment learns to use sounds to gain the same information that the non-visually impaired person gains from visual information, and therefore learns to rely more on her hearing.

Another common stereotype is that all people with a visual impairment are talented in music. The fact is that musical abilities are on a continuum: some people are very talented in music, and some are not.

If we continue to believe these myths and stereotypes, we expect the girl to do well in areas she may not enjoy and we do not allow her to develop her individual talents.

Additional myths and stereotypes associated with people with visual impairments are:

- They have extrasensory powers or are compensated by nature for their loss.
- They will damage their remaining vision by using it. Watching TV and reading will use up the sight they do have.
- Visual impairments are punishment for sin.
- A person with a visual impairment can see objects in her path by sensing them through her skin.
- Glasses will cure eye problems.
- People with visual impairments have mental retardation.
- People with visual impairments cannot hear well and must be addressed in a loud voice.

CHARACTERISTICS

The main idea in listing the following characteristics is to focus on the areas of differences and difficulty. Please keep in mind that the Girl Scout with a visual impairment is more like sighted girls her own age than she is different.

Motor Behavior

The child:

- May rock back and forth. Since she may not realize she is rocking, quietly let her know by placing your hand on her shoulder.
- May be physically weak. This weakness is not due to her visual impairment. It stems from her not being as physically active as many of the other girls.
- May not be as aware of her body as are sighted girls her own age. This is due to the lack of opportunity to clearly see her body or her reflection in a mirror.
- A visually impaired girl may use one or more of the following four ways of travel.

SIGHTED GUIDE

She may travel with a sighted person. The girl grasps the sighted guide's arm a little above the elbow. The guide's arm will remain next to the guide's body.

This places the girl a half step behind the sighted guide. The girl is able to detect, through muscles tensing and relaxing in the guide's arm, changes in the terrain such as slopes and inclines. When going up or down steps, the guide will stop at the first step and allow the girl to locate that step before starting to ascend or descend. The guide pauses when reaching the end of the stairs before starting to walk forward. If you are the sighted guide, it is important not to push or pull the girl. If you are in doubt of how to be a sighted guide, ask the girl with a visual impairment what assistance is needed.

GUIDE DOG

Some, but not all, people with visual impairments use a guide dog. Both the person and the dog have received extensive training and they work as a team. Remember that the ani-

mal is a working dog and should not be treated as a pet at troop or group meetings. When the guide dog is in its special harness, it is working and should not be spoken to or petted. A pat could distract the dog from its work. The dog with its owner can go anywhere people can go. This includes restaurants, offices, trains, or airplanes. If a Girl Scout with a visual impairment is refused entry with her guide dog, inform the management. The girl has the legal right to enter with the guide dog.

CANE TRAVEL

The most commonly used means of travel is with a white cane. The use of the white cane allows the girl with a visual impairment to maneuver more easily and participate in most activities. She may need some assistance in a crowded room, in a shopping mall, or in a dangerous setting such as a construction site. However, before giving assistance be sure to ask if help is needed or wanted.

TRAVEL ALONE

A Girl Scout who has some vision or who is familiar with a specific environment can travel with no assistance. Naturally, this form of travel allows the girl the most independence. There may be times when she will ask for help, such as in crowded rooms or on difficult surfaces. One of the most difficult surfaces to travel on is snow. Not only is footing less secure but walking on snow produces sounds different from walking on dry surfaces. Other cues are lost, such as when she is on the sidewalk and when she is not on the appropriate walkways.

The girl with a visual impairment should be as independent as possible. Know the kind of travel she uses and to what extent she can travel independently.

Learning Ability

The child:

- May have difficulty understanding something that is scenic, such as pictures or landscapes. It is difficult for her to imagine things in the visual environment. She must rely on information received from another sense organ, her ears, by someone telling her about the scene. The girl can only absorb one part of a scene at a time and must mentally put together all pieces of the description to form a picture.
- Needs actual personal experiences and information from her other sense organs. She needs to touch objects and models that girls her own age can see.
- Learns abstract concepts such as freedom and liberty at a later age than her sighted peers. This is due to her inability to use visual information and is not due to her lack of ability to learn.

There may be a large difference between how rapidly the girl with low vision learns when something is presented visually and when something is presented to her orally. When both oral and visual presentations are made, she may learn faster.

Communication Ability

The child:

- May not understand communication based on visual images.
- May not be able to read typical print.
- May read very slowly and have to reread a passage many times. The need to reread is due to her difficulty in focusing on printed material.
- Will not be able to interpret unseen or non-verbal messages such as a wink, a nod, or pointing.
- May reverse or confuse letters in words.
- May have difficulty spacing letters and words when writing. There may be spaces where they do not belong, and spaces between words may be omitted.
- May frequently lose her place while reading.
- May use special equipment to help her communicate.

Listed below is some of the equipment frequently used by people with a visual impairment.

Talking calculator: A calculator that not only displays the numbers but says the numbers out loud.

Talking computer: More like a small book, this machine allows the person to type information into it, then stores it and can play it back on request in the form of computerized speech.

Kurzweil reading machine: A large machine that reads the printed word out loud (invented by Thomas Kurzweil). This instrument would be located in a public building such as the main library in a large city.

Computer with speech: A computer program and an adapter that adds speech to a standard computer.

Braille writer: A six-key, manually operated machine that allows a person to write in Braille.

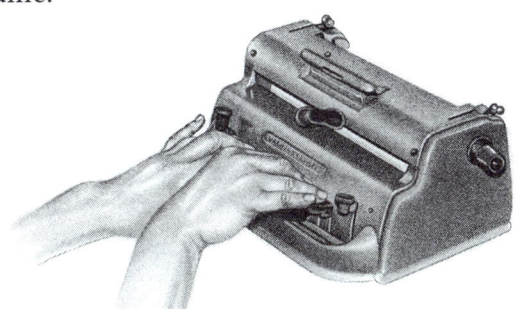

Slate and stylus: A metal frame or slate that holds Braille paper and on which a person can emboss the dots of Braille. The stylus is the instrument used to emboss the Braille dots.

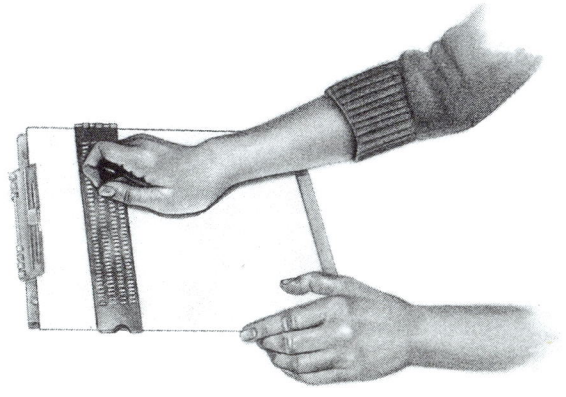

Audiotape books: Records and tapes of books for people who cannot read the printed word.

Optacon: An instrument that converts print into tactile information. The reader runs a scanner over printed material with one hand while a finger on the other hand reads the raised configurations on a small pad.

Emotional Behavior

The child:

- May express fears about doing physical activities. Because of fears held or expressed by the adults in her life, she may not have been encouraged to try new activities.
- May feel less capable than sighted girls her own age.
- May have a poor self-concept and may make negative statements about herself.

Social Behavior

The child:

- May interrupt someone who is concentrating on another activity.
- May not know when her blouse, sweater, or coat is buttoned improperly.
- May show unusual behaviors such as squinting, blinking, or frowning while listening to another person. She may have facial distortions while reading. She probably does not realize she does these things when concentrating.
- May not be aware of current social trends and styles. Example: Knowing that certain hairstyles are popular or that skirts are a certain length this year.

Sensory Characteristics

The child may change in her ability to see from day to day. Some days she will be able to see better than other days. In addition, she may grow tired much faster from reading or doing close work than sighted girls her age.

As a person working with young girls, you may observe undiagnosed eye problems. Some signs of eye problems are:

- Red eyes with crusty eyelids.
- Excessive eye rubbing.
- Difficulty reading and doing other close work.
- Inability to see distant things clearly.
- Tendency to hold work or printed material extremely close.
- Lack of interest in distant objects.

If you see a consistent pattern in any of these behaviors, be sure to notify the girl's family.

ADAPTATIONS FOR GIRLS WITH VISUAL IMPAIRMENTS

Because a visual disability influences how the Girl Scout will learn, many adaptations involve adjusting the way information and activities are presented.

Supportive Behavior

1. Girl Scout program resources are available in Braille, in large type, or on audiotape. Check the resource section of this book for ordering information, or contact your regional branch of the National Library Service for the Blind and Physically Handicapped (Library of Congress) to borrow resources. Check with your local library for information.

2. In your troop or group, use the same standards for disciplining both girls with visual impairments and nondisabled Girl Scouts. If a double standard is used, the nondisabled girl may view the girl with a visual impairment in a negative manner.

3. View the girl's visual limitation as only one part of her total self, and not the most important part.

4. Understand how important and necessary the girl's special communication equipment and materials are for learning. Examples: Braille writer, optacon, audio and tactile aids.

5. Allow the Girl Scout with a visual impairment to become familiar with the meeting room and any other setting where the troop or group will spend some time, such as a weekend campsite. Arrange for her to explore the setting in advance with a sighted guide.

6. Any needed assistance should be given in a calm and relaxed manner.

7. If a mistake or mishap occurs, it is important not to show exaggerated concern. This will have a negative effect on the girl.

8. Use words like "look" and "see" as you would with other girls. These words are also in the vocabulary of girls with visual impairments.

Communication

Below are some ideas that can assist communication.

1. When writing on a chalkboard or poster, tell the entire group what you are writing. Try not to focus on the Girl Scout with the visual impairment.

2. When talking about what you are writing, avoid the pronouns "this" and "that" when referring to something on the board. Poor example: "Put this on your paper." Good example: "Put a five-pointed star at the bottom of your paper."

3. Speak in a normal tone of voice. There is no need to talk louder or slower than usual.

4. When entering the room, be sure to call the girl's name and give your name. It is difficult for her to guess who is entering the room or who is speaking.

5. If the Girl Scout with a visual impairment enters a room where you are, let her know you are in the room.

6. Before you leave the room, be sure to tell the girl you are leaving so she will not try to talk to you after you are gone.

7. Since a Girl Scout with a visual impairment may not be able to see facial expressions, you will need to develop other means of nonverbal communication with her, such as a pat on the back.

8. If the girl drops an object, allow time for her to recover the object without any help. When assistance is needed, verbal guidance using the face of a clock can help her locate an item.

Presentation of Materials and Activities

Below are ideas to use when presenting materials.

1. In addition to having the new project or process explained orally, the Girl Scout with a visual impairment should be allowed to use her hands to examine any models or examples.

2. Avoid using material that has little contrast. There should be a great deal of contrast between the print and the background. Example: Black writing on a white background has good contrast.

3. Be sure to read out loud any directions written in a book or on paper. Give the directions in steps. This helps the girl remember the directions, since she cannot refresh her memory through sight.

4. Any new physical activity, such as a dance step, should be demonstrated by explaining and by physically moving the girl through the activity.

5. Whenever possible, new activities should be introduced through the use of materials that can be touched or handled. The Girl Scout with a visual impairment may need repeated contact with the material before learning can take place.

6. If you are showing a video, have another Girl Scout whisper the action to her.

7. When handing an object to the girl, lightly touch her hand with the object so she knows where it is located.

75

8. When the girls will be taking notes at the next troop or group meeting, tell them this in advance. The Girl Scout with a visual impairment may need to bring equipment to a meeting when information needs to be recorded for future use.

9. When speaking to the troop or group, do not stand in front of a window or other primary source of light, such as a lamp or the sun. The girl with a visual impairment will be looking at a glare and will be unable to discern images.

10. Use materials that do not have a shiny surface or produce a glare. Avoid using a table that has a shiny top.

11. Have flexible seating so the girl can move about and choose the seating position that is best for her.

12. The Girl Scout with a visual impairment should participate in as many physical activities as possible. She should not be protected from or removed from physical activity. Remember, her skinned knee does not hurt any more than a nondisabled Girl Scout's skinned knee.

Adaptation of Materials and Activities

Here are some suggestions for adapting materials and activities to help the Girl Scout with a visual impairment participate in all activities.

1. The Girl Scout with a visual impairment may need to stand or sit closer to the demonstration or model.

2. If all Girl Scouts are asked to raise their hands for attention, the Girl Scout with a visual impairment should do the same. Remember to tell her in advance any specific instructions on hand-raising or attention-getting procedures since she often cannot gain the visual cues of what other troop or group members are doing.

3. Craft activities for the girl who is visually impaired should stress the sense of touch. Suggested activities include working with clay, finger painting, weaving, paper sculpture, and collages. Perhaps the troop or group can add to this list.

4. Any drawn or printed lines should be bold and of even intensity. When giving the Girl Scout with low vision written material, you may need to go over the print with a black marking pen. This will increase the contrast and make the words easier to read. You can have the words enlarged to 18-point print.

5. When lined paper must be used for written work, use a black marking pen to darken the lines on the paper.

6. When your troop or group is taking a field trip to a museum or other exhibit, you may want to inform the management ahead of time that a Girl Scout with a visual impairment will be visiting. Often, people with visual impairments will be allowed to go beyond the barriers and touch the exhibits.

7. The Girl Scout with a visual impairment may need additional time to finish projects and activities. If the girl with a visual impairment can read any written instructions ahead of time at her own speed, it will prepare her for what will take place.

8. Project materials should be simple and uncluttered.

9. Only important information should be included in instructions.
10. The equipment and supplies should be free of sharp projections.

Memory and Organization

It is important for the girl to know her way around the meeting area and to keep her work space organized and clear. The following suggestions can help you assist her.

1. Have the girl sit so she does not face a window or a main source of light. As noted earlier, glare or bright light interferes with her ability to distinguish people and objects.
2. Give directions in steps. This helps the girl remember the directions, since she cannot refresh her memory through sight.
3. Be sure the work space for the Girl Scout with a visual impairment is large enough to hold all of her equipment, such as a Braille writer or a stylus and slate.
4. Place needed materials within her reach on the table and let her explore the work area. You can explain where items are located by relating them to the face of a clock. Example: Your pencil is at one o'clock.
5. Keep the meeting room uncluttered and free of obstacles. Things that might cause people to trip should be kept off the floor. Be sure to let the girl know of any changes in the arrangement of the room. Example: Tell her if a table or chair has been moved to a new location.
6. Be sure the doors to the room and doors to the cabinets are either completely opened or closed. Doors should never be left ajar.
7. Allow the girl to explore the building with a sighted guide to locate restrooms, water fountains, and telephones. After locations are identified, the girl can use these facilities unassisted and not be dependent on another person.
8. Make provisions for a sighted guide during fire drills and field trips.

Behavior

Some ideas for helping the Girl Scout with a visual impairment become an active member of a troop or group are:

1. When the girl interrupts a troop or group activity, quietly let her know you will answer in a moment. Encourage her to first ask if you are busy.
2. If a girl is unable to see that she has a stain on her clothing, quietly let her know and describe the location and type of stain. She may be able to change her clothing, get assistance in removing the stain, or place a safety pin on the stain for later removal.
3. If she has an unbuttoned blouse or skirt, quietly let her know and allow her to fix the clothing.
4. If the behavior of the girl is socially inappropriate, quietly and privately tell her she should not _____ in public.

FAMOUS PEOPLE

Many people who have visual impairments have been very successful. If given the opportunity to explore her or his work environment, a person with a visual disability will be able to handle most occupations. Some well-known people who have been identified as having visual impairments are listed below. You may know some people in your local community who have a visual disability. Add them to this list.

Alicia Alonso, *ballerina*
Dave Bing, *basketball player*
Ray Charles, *musician*
Sandy Duncan, *actress*
Helen Keller, *author, lecturer*
George Shearing, *musician*
Tom Sullivan, *speaker, author*
James Thurber, *author, cartoonist*
Morris Udall, *politician*
Stevie Wonder, *musician*

Chapter 10

Physical Disabilities and Health Impairments

The area of physical disabilities and health impairments includes a wide variety of disabling conditions, such as asthma, allergies, diabetes, AIDS, cerebral palsy, epilepsy, paralysis, and amputations, to name just a few. Some children may have no visible signs of an impairment while other children will use crutches, wear braces, or be in a wheelchair. With this wide variety of conditions, the needs of each individual child will also vary widely. Some girls with physical and health disabilities will need adaptations in the physical environment while others will not; some will need special adaptations in the method of communication while others will not; and some girls will need adaptation in the activities and materials used while others will not. It is important for you, the leader, to know the abilities and limitations of the girl with a physical disability or health impairment so you can provide a safe and pleasurable environment that will maximize participation.

Because of the wide variety of conditions discussed in this chapter, the organization will differ from that of the previous chapters. This chapter will be presented in two sections, physical disabilities and health impairments. For each condition there is a short description, a list of primary characteristics, and some specific adaptations. The sections on health conditions will be followed by a short description of terminal conditions. Myths and stereotypes, along with a list of famous people, are located at the end of the chapter.

PHYSICAL DISABILITIES

Amputations

There are two kinds of amputations: congenital amputations and acquired amputations. Girls with congenital amputations were born without one or more limbs. Girls with an acquired loss have had one or more limbs removed due to trauma or illness. Girls with amputations may or may not have an artificial limb or prosthesis. A girl's degree of participation in troop or group activities will depend on the age of the girl, the extent of the amputation (when more of the limb is lost, more adaptations are needed), and the girl's adjustment to the loss.

CHARACTERISTICS

The child:

- May have a poor sense of balance, which may contribute to more frequent falling.
- May move more slowly than other girls her age.
- May not attempt physical activities because of discouragement from other people or because of fear of falling.
- May show anger at not being like other girls.
- May avoid activities where the prosthesis would be obvious or more noticeable.
- May have poor posture; this will be more noticeable when the girl is fatigued.
- May tire easily.
- May have odors emitting from her missing limb.

ADAPTATIONS FOR GIRLS WITH AMPUTATIONS

1. If a child wears an artificial limb, learn the basic mechanics of the prosthesis. This information may be obtained from the child or from the child's family. Do not be afraid to ask the child for information about her artificial limb. If she prefers not to use her prosthesis, and her family agrees, allow her to participate without it. Many girls, especially those with congenital amputations, will be more comfortable without one.

2. Exercise is important for the child who has had an amputation and, therefore, should not be avoided. You may need to encourage the girl to participate. If she seems uneasy about participating, have her begin with a simple physical activity and gradually advance to more active physical activities. If she is eager to participate, however, allow her to develop her own adaptations whenever she can.

3. When there is an odor coming from her missing limb, quietly tell the girl about the odor. The area around the prosthesis may need cleaning, since little air circulates between the missing limb and the prosthesis.

4. Some girls with an amputation may need adaptive equipment such as pencil holders or page turners. Often the girl can help by telling you what types of equipment and material would be useful. You might contact the girl's schoolteacher for suggestions regarding adaptations of material and equipment.

5. It is important that you encourage and assist the girl in developing ways of compensating and adapting, rather than doing tasks for her.

Arthritis

While primarily a condition of adults, arthritis can affect young children. The most common form of arthritis in children is called juvenile rheumatoid arthritis. This condition may have a sudden onset or it may develop gradually. It may last for a short period of time such as a week, a month, a year, or it can continue throughout childhood and adult life. Arthritis attacks the joints of the body and produces pain and stiffness. The single most effective treatment is aspirin or some other anti-inflammatory medication.

CHARACTERISTICS

The child:

- May seem listless because of the effect of prescribed medication.
- May not want to participate in physical activities because of the pain.

- May be moody because of the pain or because of the effect of her medication.
- May produce work that is not as neat as expected because of the pain she experiences when moving her fingers.
- May have difficulty with activities requiring finger movement such as sewing or threading a needle.
- May take longer to complete project work.
- May tire easily.
- May seem to bleed more than expected from small cuts or scrapes.
- May walk in a stiffened manner because of the pain experienced during motion. This makes activities such as long walks or dancing very difficult for the girl with arthritis.
- May have faulty posture.
- May complain of stomach discomfort, which can be a side effect of medication.

ADAPTATIONS FOR GIRLS WITH ARTHRITIS

1. The Arthritis Foundation publishes lesson plan packets for the American Juvenile Arthritis Foundation. These packets offer information on arthritis as well as other disabilities. See the resource section for more information.
2. Since the child may experience frustration, anger, pain, and fatigue, allow for short rest periods. Also, allow the girl to express anger in appropriate ways such as talking about her feelings.
3. Since morning may be her most painful time of day, allow the girl extra time to get started in the morning on camping trips, overnights, or early morning activities.

Cerebral Palsy

Cerebral palsy is a nonprogressive condition affecting the central nervous system; it limits motor coordination.

The effects of cerebral palsy can be severe or minor. It can affect one limb, two, three, or all four limbs. In more severe cases it can affect the use of the large muscles, making walking and running difficult. In some cases, communication may also be affected.

With some adaptations, the girl with cerebral palsy should be able to participate in most activities.

CHARACTERISTICS

The child:
- May have difficulty with fine motor movements, so that activities such as writing are difficult.
- May tire easily.
- May be severely limited in her ability to communicate. Her speech may be distorted and difficult to understand. Remember that the girl will understand much more than she can communicate to you.
- May use an alternative communication system such as sign language or a communication board (a board on which one can point to symbols or words or use computerized speech) if the cerebral palsy is severe.
- May walk in a halting, jerky, or labored manner.

ADAPTATIONS FOR GIRLS WITH CEREBRAL PALSY

1. Remember that the girl with speech difficulties may be very bright. When talking with her, use language that matches her understanding, not her speech.
2. Maintain good eye contact while listening to the girl whose speech is affected by cerebral palsy. This eye contact will tell the girl that what she has to say is important.
3. If the girl uses a different communication system, make an effort to learn that system. This would help her become an active participant in the troop or group and, at the same time, increase the other girls' understanding of the condition.
4. The girl may need to use a keyboard guard when using a typewriter. This is a specially designed plate that helps keep the fingers from slipping off the keys while typing.

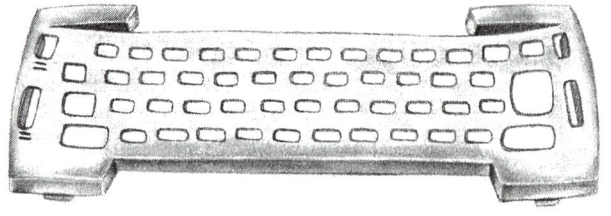

5. If the cerebral palsy is severe, the child may use adapted eating utensils. Ask the girl or her parents if special utensils are necessary.

Spina Bifida

Spina bifida is a birth defect in which the bones of the spine fail to close during development of the fetus. The degree of disability can range from little or no effect to varying degrees of paralysis of the legs. If the defect is above the area on the spinal cord that controls the bowel and the bladder, the girl may be incontinent. This child may wear a bag that receives and holds her urine.

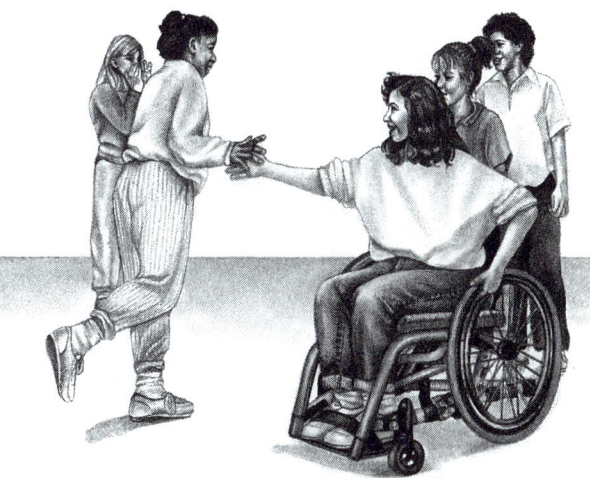

CHARACTERISTICS

The child:

- May or may not be in a wheelchair or wear braces.
- May have a poor self-concept and feel she is not able to participate in some activities.
- May lack some social skills because of not having had the opportunity to experience some very common things such as grocery shopping or eating in a restaurant.
- May have poor muscle strength and tone in parts of her body due to her lack of exercise and the lack of encouragement to participate in physical activities.
- May be unaware of cuts and bruises on her legs because of loss of feeling due to nerve damage.
- May not know when her bladder is full because of damage affecting these nerve fibers; this can result in overflow and wet clothing.
- May become the brunt of jokes if she has urine odor due to bladder leakage. When explaining to the other girls, be sure to give the physical reasons for this condition.

ADAPTATIONS FOR GIRLS WITH SPINA BIFIDA

1. Encourage the girl with spina bifida to take a leadership role in her troop or group. This can begin with activities in which she is skilled, such as music, public speaking, or archery.

2. Exercise is very important for the girl's muscles. This will help maintain good muscle tone in the upper part of her body. In addition, exercise helps maintain good circulation in the total body. Ask both the girl and her family about the appropriate amounts and types of exercise allowed.

3. Do not assume that the girl with spina bifida is familiar with common activities. Include her in even the simplest project such as shopping for a camping trip.

4. Watch for cuts and scrapes that she may not feel and administer appropriate first aid.

5. If wetness or an odor is evident, quietly tell the girl about it and assist her in changing her clothing or correcting the problem.

6. If the other girls make fun of her because of the odor or wetness, have a nurse or someone from the medical profession speak to the group about spina bifida. It is important that the other girls do not feel sorry for her but understand the problem so they will accept the girl and be supportive of her.

Other Physical Disabilities

Some girls with disabilities such as dwarfism, gigantism, etc., will be able to participate in almost any activity they choose. However, everyday items such as tables, chairs, bookshelves, and counters may present barriers. A girl may also face other problems, such as finding a uniform that fits. By discussing with the girls and her family some of the adaptations she needs, you can help make her participation in activities much easier.

Adaptations That Apply to All Physical Disabilities

SUPPORTIVE BEHAVIOR

1. Encourage independence in a positive manner. A lessening of dependence will help create a positive self-concept. Asking the girl with a physical disability to help you or the other girls is a good technique.
2. Before trying to make an adaptation, ask the girl how you can help. She will be able to suggest adaptations that will help her to participate fully in the group activities.
3. Do not overreact to a fall. Before rushing to assist the girl, inquire if she is injured. If she is not hurt, allow time for her to rise unaided before you assist her. This encourages independent behavior.
4. If one or more of the girl's items fall on the floor, observe whether she tries to pick them up before you assist. Independence should always be encouraged.
5. If the girl uses a wheelchair, do not be too quick to push the chair for her. She may prefer to be as independent as possible and move her own wheelchair. Self-management of a wheelchair should be encouraged.

6. Before planning a visit, inquire if the building is barrier-free. If it is not, plan to obtain assistance in moving the girl who is physically limited, or choose a different activity. If the building is a public one, such as a courthouse or library, you might request assistance from the manager of the building.
7. Allow for short rest periods, since fatigue may be a problem.
8. When poor posture is exhibited, quietly remind the girl about proper sitting or standing posture.
9. If the girl has difficulty managing a cup or a glass, be careful not to completely fill any container. A cup two-thirds full is much easier to handle than a full cup.

ADAPTATION OF MATERIALS AND ACTIVITIES

1. Schedule quiet times for everyone in the troop to rest and talk quietly.
2. Allow alternatives to written projects. Use audiotapes or cameras to replace written work.
3. Allow more time for projects. This can be done by allowing the girl to start an activity earlier, or by allowing her to finish at a later date.

4. For a task that requires fine hand movement, use an adaptation to make gripping easier. Examples: A shower curtain ring will make a book bag zipper easier to open and close. Push pins inserted in items will assist the girl in picking up material by herself.

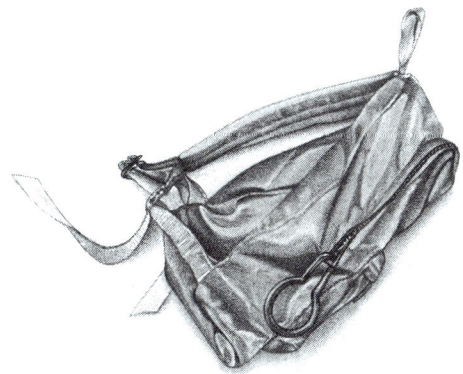

5. Add handles to help with lifting and holding items. Example: Rope loops allow for easier gripping.

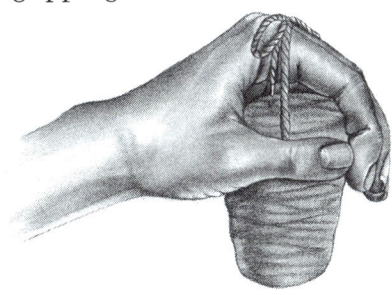

6. Have the girl carry small items in a backpack or a shoulder bag.

7. A basket or book bag attached to a wheelchair will help the girl to independently manage her materials.

8. Fine-line pens that require little exertion of pressure when writing may be easier to handle.

9. Pencil holders made of clay or even sponges can help the girl who has difficulty with fine motor movements. Pencil grippers, sold at bookstores or stationery stores, can also help.

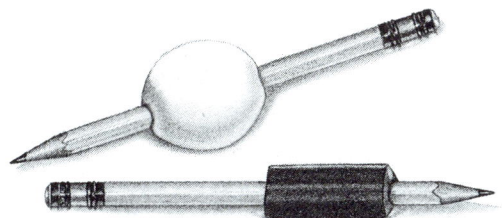

10. Page turners may also be useful for the girl who has a fine motor disability.

11. There are many ways to adapt games so all can play:
    - The number of points to finish the game can be reduced.
    - The game can be divided into quarters or halves. These breaks will give enforced periods of rest and allow for rotation of players.
    - Additional players can be added to each team.

- Use larger or softer equipment, or add handles to equipment where helpful. Use yarn balls or sponge balls to make catching and throwing easier for the girl with limited motor ability.
- Make the size of the playing area smaller.
- Minor rule changes can be made while retaining as many as possible of the basic rules of the game.

PRESENTATION OF MATERIALS AND ACTIVITIES

1. When presenting materials or examples of work, be sure to hold items at the eye level of the girl in a wheelchair.

2. Since the girl with limited motor ability cannot physically move around a model or example, place the model where the girl can touch it and turn it around.

COMMUNICATION

If the girl has limited communication ability or uses an alternative communication system, it is important that you initiate communication with her. Make an effort to learn the system she uses. When she is speaking, look directly at her face. Do not anticipate and do not finish sentences for her.

WORK SPACE

1. Her desk or table should be of a height that allows the girl to sit comfortably with her arms resting on the table or countertop.

2. See that needed materials are within the reach of the girl in a wheelchair.

3. If a child has a prosthesis, the height of her work surface should be adjusted to complement its functioning.

4. See that passageways are clear so that the girl in a wheelchair or a girl with braces or crutches can move around the room independently.

5. Position the girl in a wheelchair at the table so that the arms of her chair are under the table. If the chair arms will not fit under the table, obtain a lapboard for the girl to use. Do not, however, have her sit by herself. Be sure to include her in the group around the table.

6. Develop ways to steady work materials being used. An embroidery hoop can be used to hold or smooth out fabric or to retain small objects.

7. Objects, such as a small box or jar, can be affixed to the surface of a table or desk by using two-sided tape or by attaching a loop of standard tape to the bottom of the item. (See next page.) This will help keep needed items within reach and prevent their falling to the floor.

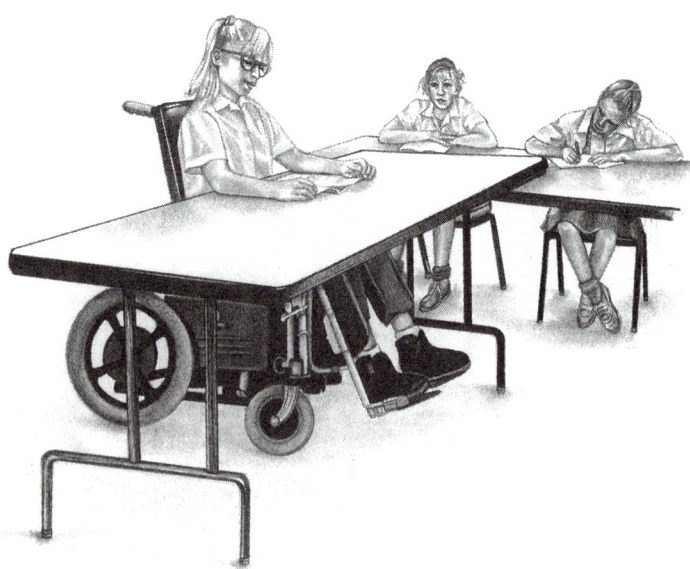

8. Paper holders or book holders can be helpful for girls who have the use of only one arm or have very limited use of both arms.

9. A clipboard or a piece of tape will hold the girl's paper in place while she is working.

10. Using a ruler as a bookmark will help the girl to independently open and close her book.

11. Use a long string to tie a pencil to her seat or to the arm of her wheelchair. This will allow the girl to retrieve it if it is dropped.

12. If the girl has limited use of her arms or hands, a rim around the edge of the table may keep things from rolling off the surface.

SOCIAL BEHAVIOR

1. When the behavior of the girl is immature, quietly inform her that her behavior is inappropriate and give her some suggested alternative behaviors.

2. If her lower limbs are affected, the girl may need extra time to move from one place to another. If the group is walking together, slow the pace so all can stay together. Another idea is to divide into two groups, a slow group and a fast group. Be sure there is a leader with both groups. A third idea is to allow the girl who has difficulty walking to depart with an adult ahead of time.

3. Encourage group activities. This will increase the number of opportunities in which the girl with limited physical ability can participate.

HEALTH IMPAIRMENTS

Health impairments are physical conditions that alter a portion of a person's life habits but may not be readily observable to others.

Allergies

An allergy is an adverse sensitivity or intolerance to a substance. A person's reaction when she comes into contact with the substance can take many forms, including sneezing, watery eyes, runny nose, rash, or swollen body tissue. Some reactions are minor and some are serious and life-threatening. A girl may have reactions to several different substances. Examples of some common irritants are:

- Inhalants: pollen, paint fumes, smoke, dust, perfume.
- Food.
- Bacteria or fungi, such as mold or mildew.
- Substances that come into contact with the skin, such as poison ivy or grass.
- Stings and bites.
- Drugs.
- Animal hair, fur.

CHARACTERISTICS

The child:

- May be afraid to try new foods for fear of an allergic reaction.
- May be listless and appear disinterested due to her allergy medication.
- May be afraid of physical activity even when the activity does not relate to her allergic reaction.
- May attempt to use the allergy to avoid new activities.
- May be immature in her social development because she has missed a great deal of school.
- May be physically weak due to lack of physical exercise.
- May tire easily and need frequent rest periods.
- May be socially and emotionally withdrawn from the group.

ADAPTATIONS FOR GIRLS WITH ALLERGIES

1. *For food allergies:* Know which foods produce allergic reactions, and check the ingredient listings for all foods to be served. When helping girls plan a menu, be sure to include foods all the girls can eat. Plan substitutes that are pleasant. If a girl cannot eat chocolate, have another dessert for her. Another solution is to have choices for all girls. If everyone has choices, then no individual girl is singled out.

2. *For nonfood substances:* It is critical to know which substances cause an allergic reaction and the necessary procedures and medication in case there is an adverse reaction.

3. Know whether the girl is taking any medicine to prevent an adverse reaction and her schedule for taking medication.

4. Encourage participation in all activities unless restrictions are appropriate because of the allergy.

5. If the child appears fatigued, allow for short rest periods.

Diabetes

Diabetes is a metabolic disorder in which the body does not properly use or store sugar. This condition can become dangerous if proper treatment procedures are not followed. A person with diabetes will use one or both of the following treatments.

1. The person may be on a controlled diet.
2. The person may take some form of medication orally or by injection on a regular basis.

Listed below are two situations of which you, the leader, must be aware.

INSULIN SHOCK (HYPOGLYSEMIA)

Insulin shock can be brought on by an imbalance of sugar and insulin due to too much exercise, too much insulin, too little food, or nervous tension.

When a child fails to eat a meal, the body's insulin level becomes imbalanced by the lack of food intake and insulin shock can result. Signs of impending insulin shock are malaise, excessive thirst, excessive perspiration, nausea, vomiting, frequent urination.

Each girl will exhibit different signs of insulin shock; some girls will experience all of the symptoms, and some girls will experience only a few of the symptoms. Before there is a problem, you will need to learn the procedures for treatment from the girl's parents. Many times the treatment will be fruit juice. Do not, however, administer anything without knowledge of the appropriate treatment.

It is critical to notify the girl's family of any changes that have occurred in her behavior.

DIABETIC COMA

A diabetic coma is produced when the level of sugar in the body is so high that the body cannot function properly. It is usually caused by failure to take medication or failure to maintain a proper diet. Precursors to a diabetic coma are excessive thirst, frequent urination, labored breathing, nausea, or vomiting.

Observation of any of the above signs should be reported to the child's parents as soon as possible. Treatment involves rest and medication prescribed by the girl's physician.

With appropriate medication and/or modification in diet, the girl with diabetes can be expected to participate in all activities.

CHARACTERISTICS

The child:
- May be on a strict diet.
- May not follow the proper diet because of social pressure.
- May be on self-medication; this may be either oral or by injection.
- May need a place to keep medication refrigerated during long meetings or events and on overnights.
- May have sores that heal slowly.
- May be moody as her blood sugar level rises and falls.
- May fatigue easily.
- May need to urinate frequently.

ADAPTATIONS FOR GIRLS WITH DIABETES

Be sure your assistant leader is also aware of appropriate adaptations.

1. Check with the child's family to see what foods are appropriate. If the child needs a snack mid-morning or mid-afternoon, find out what snacks are appropriate.
2. Avoid excessive physical activities right before a meal.
3. Allow the child flexible use of the restroom.
4. Do not draw attention to any difference in physical restrictions or diet.
5. Avoid pampering the girl or otherwise drawing attention to her.
6. Encourage the child with diabetes to follow her diet and medication schedule.
7. Make sure she has access to required medications or snacks at all times.

Epilepsy

Epilepsy is a symptom of an underlying disorder in the nervous system. Many girls with epilepsy take medication that affects their central nervous system, and must take it on a regular schedule.

Seizures are the primary sign of all types of epilepsy. There are several types of seizures, as described below. For many girls, medication can control the seizures most or all of the time.

GENERALIZED TONIC-CLONIC (GRAND MAL) SEIZURES

This type of seizure often starts with a cry caused by air suddenly forced from the lungs. During a generalized tonic-clonic seizure the individual loses consciousness and the muscles become stiff and rigid. The girl may lose control of her bladder, she may bite her tongue, and her complexion may become bluish or pale. Following the seizure the child may be confused, drowsy, and not able to recall what happened. The seizure will usually last from one minute to five minutes.

Steps to take in the event of a generalized tonic-clonic seizure are:

1. Remain calm. The other girls will follow your lead. If possible, have the girls continue their activity. This will prevent the group from gathering, watching, and becoming frightened. When you remain calm, it lessens the other girls' fear of seizures and helps develop an accepting attitude toward the girl with epilepsy.
2. Do not restrain the girl. Nothing you do can stop a seizure once it has begun.
3. Help the child lie down on her side and put something soft such as a coat or blanket under her head.
4. Any objects on which the child might injure herself should be moved out of the way. Example: Move the table from over the girl. Do not try to pull the girl out from under the table.
5. Remove eyeglasses and any tight clothing such as a neck scarf or belt.
6. Do not force anything between the girl's teeth or into her mouth.
7. After the seizure has run its course, turn the girl's head to one side to aid release of saliva.
8. Do not allow the girl to drink any fluid until she is fully alert and responsive.
9. Allow the girl to rest following the seizure.
10. Call her parents and inform them of the seizure.
11. If the other girls ask questions, answer factually. Do not treat the questions in a hush-hush manner. A nurse or other person in the medical profession can attend a meeting and speak on the condition of epilepsy. Be sure to treat epilepsy as a condition and not a disease.

ABSENCE (PETIT MAL) SEIZURES

Absence seizures are seizures of short duration lasting only two seconds to a minute; they frequently go undetected. During this type of seizure, the girl may seem to be daydreaming or just staring into space. The child loses contact with what is going on in the room but does not lose consciousness. After the seizure, the girl will continue what she was doing and may know she has had a seizure. She may not, however, know what happened in the room during the seizure.

Signs of absence seizure are:

- Head drooping.
- Appearance of daydreaming.
- Lack of attentiveness.
- Slight jerky movements of the arms.
- Getting directions confused or not knowing complete directions.
- Eye blinking.
- Chewing motions.
- Dropping things frequently.

As a leader, your attitude and your response during and following an absence seizure are very important. When the girl asks questions or seems to have missed some information, repeat the missed information for the entire group without drawing attention to the girl or punishing her. Another alternative is to quietly go to her and repeat any information she may have missed.

ATONIC/AKINETIC (DROP) SEIZURES

During this type of seizure, there is a very brief loss of muscle tone accompanied by an equally brief loss of consciousness. With the loss of muscle tone, the girl will suddenly become limp and fall to the ground. Although the seizure may be over in a matter of seconds, and the girl will be able to get up and resume activities, she may acquire cuts and bruises during the fall. For this reason, some girls with atonic/akinetic seizures may wear helmets to protect their face and forehead. Since these seizures are so brief, the best support you can offer is to ensure she wears her helmet if she has one, and to attend to any cuts or scrapes as necessary. Also inform her parents ahead of time if the girls will be engaging in activities that are more active than usual.

MYOCLONIC SEIZURES

These seizures are characterized by sudden muscle movements that may involve a sudden forward jerking of the head, upward movement of both arms, or sudden jerking of the entire body. If the movement is severe, the girl may fall, but these seizures usually only last a few seconds. A girl may have several of these seizures a day, but usually will not become drowsy, nor will she usually need much assistance.

One type of myoclonic seizure is called "status epilepticus." This refers to a seizure that lasts more than thirty minutes, or to a series of seizures that occur without much time in between. Although this situation is rare, it is life-threatening. When it does occur, the girl should be taken immediately to an emergency room.

With an accepting attitude by you and group members, adaptations are minor for a girl with epilepsy. As the leader you need to be aware of any medication she may be taking, any situations that might increase the probability of a seizure, and any specific limitations such as not being able to ride a bike, drive an automobile, or go on amusement rides.

Attention Deficit Disorder/Attention Deficit Hyperactivity Disorder (ADD/ADHD)

Two disorders seen in children of school age are attention deficit disorder (ADD) and attention deficit hyperactivity disorder (ADHD). Attention deficit disorder is a term used to describe the lack of ability to attend to a task. Attention deficit hyperactivity disorder refers to the inability to pay attention to a task, along with a tendency to have a high rate of purposeless movement. Some girls may jump from task to task. Many times girls will not finish projects or activities because they become interested in something else. The girls will not remain at any task for a long period of time. With ADHD, the girl not only has difficulty staying with a project or task, she will be moving around even when there is a quiet activity.

ADD and ADHD are conditions that are confirmed only by physicians. A girl with ADD/ADHD may be on medication that affects her central nervous system and should be taken on a regular schedule. Some girls are taken off their medication on weekends or school holidays, and may have difficulty if Girl Scout activities are held during those times. It is not appropriate to insist that a girl take medication, but you may want to discuss with her family the types of activities planned so that they can consult the girl's doctor.

Remember that the girl is not trying to misbehave intentionally, so chastising her will not be helpful. She can, however, learn to develop her social skills with your help. Routines and structure will help her modify disruptive behavior, while careful attention to any special dietary needs and rest breaks will help her physically. Refer to the chapters on learning disabilities and behavior disorders for more specific suggestions.

Heart Disorders

There are two major types of heart disorders: congenital and acquired. In a congenital heart disorder, the damage to the heart occurred before birth. With an acquired heart disorder, the girl was born with a normal heart and due to infection or trauma the heart was damaged. The most common acquired heart disorder is caused by rheumatic fever. Many heart disorders, both acquired and congenital, can be corrected by surgery or medication that allows the girl to lead a normal life.

CHARACTERISTICS

The child:
- May be physically weak due to her lack of physical activity.
- May be afraid of physical activity.
- May fatigue easily and require more rest periods.
- May be socially immature if she was not allowed or encouraged to participate in activities when she was a young child or has had a lack of social interaction due to frequent hospitalizations.

ADAPTATIONS FOR GIRLS WITH A HEART DISORDER

1. Consult with the girl's parents concerning appropriate expectations, precautions, and any prescribed medication.
2. If the child is allowed limited physical activity, plan additional activities with less physical stress and allow all the girls to choose among the activities.

3. Allow for short rest periods for all girls.
4. Plan some group activities that require only limited physical activity. This will help the child with a heart disorder to learn to play and interact in a group situation. It is important that she be an active participant in the plans of the troop or group and not be a bystander.

Cystic Fibrosis

Cystic fibrosis is an error in metabolism causing mucus in the body to be thick and sticky. This thick mucus clogs in the bronchial tubes, making breathing difficult, and can lead to lung damage.

CHARACTERISTICS

The child:

- May cough frequently. This cough is not contagious and there is no need to keep the other troop or group members away from her.
- May not have the physical stamina of other girls the same age.
- May attempt to hide the condition by over-exerting herself.
- May be socially immature due to frequent hospitalizations and absences from school.

ADAPTATIONS FOR GIRLS WITH CYSTIC FIBROSIS

1. As with all health impairments, check with the child's parents to identify expectations, precautions, and prescribed medications.
2. Have a flexible restroom policy so that the girl with cystic fibrosis (who is likely to cough frequently) will feel free to leave the room as necessary.
3. When an activity is physically exerting, plan to have short breaks. Also, rotate tasks or roles within the activity so the girl with cystic fibrosis can select an activity that is less active and still continue to participate.
4. Care must be taken not to overprotect the girl.

Asthma

Asthma, in most cases, is the result of an allergic state that causes an obstruction of the bronchial tubes or lungs or both. Breathing becomes difficult when there is an allergic reaction. An excessive amount of mucus is produced and there are spasms of the muscles surrounding the bronchial tubes. An attack can last for minutes or for hours.

These attacks can cause emotional stress not only for the girl experiencing the attack but for the other girls. A highly emotional state may increase the frequency and severity of the attacks. Remaining calm during an attack is critical.

Most girls with asthma will be monitored by a doctor on an ongoing basis. They may be prescribed particular treatments such as inhalers or medication, periods of rest, or a combination of procedures. Make sure the girl has ready access to her inhaler and sits upright when she has trouble breathing, takes any medication on schedule, and refrains from prolonged physical activity, particularly in extreme weather conditions. Have specific recommendations from her doctor on hand.

CHARACTERISTICS

The child:

- May be afraid to try physical activity for fear of an asthma attack.
- May use the threat of an asthma attack to avoid work or other physical exertion.
- May be withdrawn from the group and need encouragement to participate in group activities.
- May wheeze or cough frequently. The cough is not contagious and she should not be kept away from the other girls.
- May be absent from school frequently. Therefore, she may seem shy or withdrawn in comparison with other girls.

ADAPTATIONS FOR GIRLS WITH ASTHMA

1. Contact the parents to identify appropriate procedures during and following an asthma attack.
2. Create a positive and nonthreatening environment.
3. Try to lessen emotional stress by not creating competitive situations.
4. When the girl's social behavior is immature, quietly inform her and suggest an appropriate alternative behavior.

Terminal Illnesses

Three types of terminal illnesses are discussed briefly below, followed by a discussion of adaptations for girls with terminal illnesses.

LEUKEMIA

Leukemia is a malignancy of the bone marrow that causes a large overproduction of white blood cells. The most common treatment for leukemia is chemotherapy.

A child with leukemia may have a puffy appearance while on chemotherapy. In addition, she may experience loss of hair and become overweight. The girl will tire easily and miss a great deal of school due to the chemotherapy and the effects of the leukemia.

MUSCULAR DYSTROPHY

Muscular dystrophy is a progressive and continuous weakening of the body's voluntary muscles. Over a period of time the child is increasingly unable to use her legs and arms. She may develop a swayback appearance and exhibit increasing clumsiness in walking. Frequent falls are common. This is followed by inability to walk, which will confine the child to a wheelchair. Slowly the girl will lose her ability to use all muscles.

ACQUIRED IMMUNE DEFICIENCY SYNDROME (AIDS)

Acquired immune deficiency syndrome is caused by the human immuno-deficiency virus (HIV), leading to a breakdown in the immune system. HIV is only transmitted through blood or bodily fluids. Latex gloves should be worn when treating an open wound, just as they would for someone who has not been diagnosed with HIV or AIDS. Remember, however, that the girl with HIV/AIDS is always more at risk of catching someone else's disease than she is of passing hers along. Be sure to notify her family if you think she has been exposed to a cold, the flu, measles, chicken pox, or any other contagious diseases. Activities may need to be adapted to prevent fatiguing or physical stress. Refer to *Safety-Wise* for more information.

ADAPTATIONS FOR GIRLS WITH A TERMINAL ILLNESS

1. Create a positive and comfortable place to be with friends. It should be rewarding to come to the Girl Scout meeting.

2. Encourage the girl to participate in all activities where she is able. The troop or group should not eliminate her from activities. Set up activities so she can be as independent as possible.

3. Keep in contact with the girl even when she can no longer attend meetings regularly. Let her know she is a member of the troop or group regardless of the number of meetings she can attend.

4. With some illnesses, such as leukemia and AIDS, the body's immune system may be weakened, and even a simple cold can become serious. Discuss with all parents how important it is to keep girls at home if they have a contagious illness of any kind, so that all girls are less at risk. If you will be on a field trip or at an event where you are not sure about what the girl may be exposed to, discuss with her parents or guardians any precautions they feel are necessary.

5. Have other girls assume responsibility for keeping her informed of the troop or group activities when she is absent.

6. Be open and honest about terminal illness and death. Have a social worker or nurse skilled in working with the terminally ill visit the troop or group and discuss with the other girls what they can do to help understand their feelings and the feelings of the girl who is terminally ill.

MYTHS AND STEREOTYPES

As with all disabling conditions, myths and stereotypes may prevent people from knowing the talents of each person and accepting her as an individual. Some common false beliefs about people with physical disabilities or health impairments are that they:

- Are being punished for their sins.
- Should not be employed because they will have an accident or cause an embarrassing scene.
- Should not get married or have children because they cannot take care of children.
- Are possessed by evil spirits.
- Are retarded and should be in an institution.
- Are dangerous.
- (Epilepsy) Will swallow their tongue when they have a seizure.
- (HIV/AIDS) Can spread the disease by sharing food, touching, or just being around someone.

FAMOUS PEOPLE

Many famous people have had a physical or health disability. Listed below are a few names. Have the girls in the troop or group add to the list.

Physical Disabilities

    Jim Abbott, *baseball player*
    Jane Addams, *social worker, Nobel Prize winner*
    Daria Alinovi, *athlete, model*
    Sarah Bernhardt, *actress*
    Roy Campanella, *baseball player, speaker, author*
    Al Capp, *cartoonist*
    Tom Dempsey, *football player*
    Robert Dole, *politician*
    Jane Froman, *singer*
    Stephen Hawking, *scientist, author*
    Linda Hunt, *actress*
    Ivey Hunter, *model, motivational speaker*
    Daniel Inouye, *politician*
    Geri Jewell, *comedian*
    Barbara Jordan, *politician*
    Dorothea Lange, *photographer*
    Carlos May, *athlete*
    Christopher Nolan, *poet, author*
    Itzhak Perlman, *violinist*
    Christopher Reeve, *actor, director*
    Franklin Delano Roosevelt, *U.S. President*
    Wilma Rudolph, *Olympic athlete*
    Joni Eareckson Tada, *author, artist*
    Bree Walker, *broadcast journalist*
    George Wallace, *politician*

Health Disabilities

    Lola Falana, *entertainer*
    Annette Funicello, *entertainer*
    Elizabeth Glaser, *activist*
    Andrew Jackson, *U.S. President*
    Magic Johnson, *athlete, activist*
    Jackee Joyner-Kersee, *Olympic athlete*
    Naomi Judd, *singer*
    Mary Tyler Moore, *actress*
    Flannery O'Connor, *author*
    Harriett Tubman, *nineteenth-century political activist*

Appendix

OVERVIEW OF ADA, IDEA, AND SECTION 504

Americans with Disabilities Act of 1990 (ADA)	Individuals with Disabilities Education Act (IDEA)	Section 504 of the Rehabilitation Act of 1973
Type/Purpose		
A civil rights law to prohibit discrimination solely on the basis of disability in employment, public services, and accommodations.	An education act to provide federal financial assistance to state and local education agencies to guarantee special education and related services to eligible children with disabilities.	A civil rights law to prohibit discrimination on the basis of disability in programs and activities, public and private, that receive federal financial assistance.
Who Is Protected?		
Any individual with a disability who: (1) has a physical or mental impairment that substantially limits one or more life activities, or (2) has a record of such an impairment, or (3) is regarded as having such an impairment. Further, the person must be qualified for the program, service, or job.	Children ages 3–21 who are determined by a multidisciplinary team to be eligible within one or more of 13 specific disability categories and who need special education and related services. Categories include autism, deafness, deaf-blindness, hearing impairments, mental retardation, multiple disabilities, orthopedic impairments, other health impairments, serious emotional disturbance, specific learning disabilities, speech or language impairments, traumatic brain injury, and visual impairments.	Any person who: (1) has a physical or mental impairment that substantially limits one or more major life activities, or (2) has a record of such an impairment, or (3) is regarded as having such an impairment. Major life activities include walking, seeing, hearing, speaking, breathing, learning, working, caring for oneself, and performing manual tasks.

Americans with Disabilities Act of 1990 (ADA)	Individuals with Disabilities Education Act (IDEA)	Section 504 of the Rehabilitation Act of 1973

Responsibility to Provide a Free, Appropriate Public Education (FAPE)?

Not directly. However, (1) ADA protections apply to nonsectarian private schools, but not to organizations or entities controlled by religious organizations; (2) ADA provides additional protection in combination with actions brought under Section 504 and IDEA. Reasonable accommodations are required for eligible students with a disability to perform essential functions of a job. This applies to any part of the special education program that may be community-based and involve job training/placement.	Yes. A FAPE is defined to mean special education and related services. Special education means "specially designed instruction, at no cost to the parents, to meet the unique needs of the child with a disability...." Related services are provided if students require them in order to benefit from specially designed instruction. States are required to ensure the provision of "full educational opportunity" to all children with disabilities. IDEA requires the development of an Individualized Education Program (IEP) document with specific content and a required number of specific participants at an IEP meeting.	Yes. An "appropriate" education means an education comparable to that provided to students without disabilities. This may be defined as regular or special education services. Students can receive related services under Section 504 even if they are not provided any special education. Section 504 does require development of a plan, although this written document is not mandated. The Individualized Education Program (IEP) of IDEA may be used for the Section 504 written plan. Many experts recommend that a group of persons knowledgeable about the students convene and specify the agreed-upon services.

Funding to Implement Requirements?

No, but limited tax credits may be available for removing architectural or transportation barriers. Also, many federal agencies provide grant funds to support training and to provide technical assistance to public and private institutions.	Yes. IDEA provides federal funds under Parts B and H to assist states and local education agencies in meeting IDEA requirements to serve infants, toddlers, children, and youth with disabilities.	No. State and local jurisdictions have responsibility. IDEA funds may not be used to serve children found eligible only under Section 504.

Americans with Disabilities Act of 1990 (ADA)	Individuals with Disabilities Education Act (IDEA)	Section 504 of the Rehabilitation Act of 1973

Procedural Safeguards

The ADA does not specify procedural safeguards related to special education; it does detail the administrative requirements, complaint procedures, and the consequences for noncompliance, related to both services and employment.	IDEA requires written notice to parents regarding identification, evaluation, and/or placement. Further, written notice must be made prior to any change in placement. The Act delineates the required components of the written notices.	Section 504 requires notice to parents regarding identification, evaluation, and/or placement. Written notice is recommended. Notice must be made only before a "significant change" in placement. Following IDEA procedural safeguards is one way to meet Section 504 mandates.

Evaluation/Placement Procedures

The ADA does not specify evaluation and placement procedures; it does specify provision of reasonable accommodations for eligible students across educational activities and settings. Reasonable accommodations may include, but are not limited to, redesigning equipment, assigning aides, providing written communication in alternative formats, modifying tests, redesigning services to accessible locations, altering existing facilities, and building new facilities.	A comprehensive evaluation is required. A multidisciplinary team evaluates the child, and parental consent is required before an initial evaluation. IDEA requires that reevaluations be conducted at least every 3 years. A reevaluation is not required before a significant change in placement. For evaluation and placement decisions, IDEA requires that more than one single procedure or information source be used; that information from all sources be documented and carefully considered; that the eligibility decision be made by a group of persons who know about the student, the evaluation data, and placement options; and that the placement decision serves the student in the least restrictive environment. An IEP review meeting is required before any change in placement.	Unlike IDEA, Section 504 requires only notice, not consent, for evaluation. It is recommended that districts obtain parental consent. Like IDEA, evaluation and placement procedures under Section 504 require that information be obtained from a variety of sources in the area of concern; that all data are documented and considered; and that decisions are made by a group of persons knowledgeable about the student, evaluation data, and placement options. Section 504 requires periodic reevaluations, but does not specify any timelines for placement. Section 504 requires that students be educated with their nondisabled peers to the maximum extent appropriate. Section 504 does not require a meeting for any change in placement.

Americans with Disabilities Act of 1990 (ADA)	Individuals with Disabilities Education Act (IDEA)	Section 504 of the Rehabilitation Act of 1973

Due Process

The ADA does not delineate specific due process procedures. People with disabilities have the same remedies that are available under Title VII of the Civil Rights Act of 1964, as amended in 1991. Thus, individuals who are discriminated against may file a complaint with the relevant federal agency or sue in federal court. Enforcement agencies encourage informal mediation and voluntary compliance.	IDEA delineates specific requirements for local education agencies to provide impartial hearings for parents who disagree with the identification, evaluation, or placement of a child.	Section 504 requires local education agencies to provide impartial hearings for parents who disagree with the identification, evaluation, or placement of a student. It requires that parents have an opportunity to participate in the hearing process and to be represented by counsel. Beyond this, due process details are left to the discretion of the local education agency. It is recommended that districts develop policy guidance and procedures.

Resource Information

The following resources can help girls and adults understand both the behaviors and the feelings of girls with disabilities. When reviewing books, either yourself or with girls, analyze the characters and attitudes portrayed. Is the person with a disability depicted as someone to be pitied, or as equal to his or her peers? Do the characters sometimes have "superhuman powers," or does it take their saving someone's life to be accepted? Is the disability the defining characteristic of the character, or just one attribute? You may want to discuss with girls the images portrayed in books and the media of people with disabilities.

In addition to the lists of books for girls and adults, a section on games, kits, videos, and manuals is provided, followed by the names and national addresses of organizations that can provide additional resource information. To obtain listings of local offices for these organizations, contact the national offices or check your local telephone book. It is hoped that use of these resources will increase the understanding, acceptance, and participation of girls with disabilities.

BOOKS FOR GIRLS

Aiello, Barbara, and Jeffrey Shulman. *The Kids on the Block Book Series*. Frederick, Md.: Twenty-first Century Books, 1989.

American Brain Tumor Association. *Alex's Journey: The Story of a Child with a Brain Tumor*. Des Plains, Ill.: Author, 1994.

Ancona, George, and Mary Beth Miller. *Handtalk School*. New York: Four Winds Press, Maxwell MacMillan International, 1991.

Anderson, Rachel. *The Bus People*. New York: Henry Holt, 1992.

Axline, Virginia. *Dibs: In Search of Self*. New York: Ballantine, 1976. (Also good for adults.)

Baker, Pamela J. *My First Book of Sign*. Washington, D.C.: Gallaudet University Press, 1986.

Behrman, Carol H. *Fiddler to the World: The Inspiring Story of Itzhak Perlman*. White Hall, Va.: Shoe Tree Press, 1992.

Berger, Larry, Dahlia Lithwick, and Robert Benson (ill.). *I Will Sing Life: Voices from the Hole in the Wall Gang Camp*. Boston: Little, Brown, 1992.

Bergman, Thomas. *On Our Own Terms: Children Living with Physical Disabilities*. Milwaukee, Wis.: Gareth Stevens Children's Books, 1989.

Berkus, Clara W. *Charlsie's Chuckle*. Rockville, Md.: Woodbine House, 1992.

Betancourt, Jeanne. *My Name Is Brain-Brian*. New York: Scholastic, 1993.

Buckle, Marian C., and Tiffany Buckle. *Mom, I Have a Staring Problem: A True Story of Petit Mal Seizures and the Hidden Problem It Can Cause: Learning Disability*. Bradenton, Fla.: Author, 1992.

Calvert, Patricia. *Picking Up the Pieces*. New York: Scribner's, Maxwell MacMillan International, 1993.

Campanella, Roy. *It's Good to Be Alive*. Boston: Little, Brown, 1959.

Charles, R., and S. Mathis, *Ray Charles*. New York: Thomas Y. Crowell, 1975.

Charlip, R., and M. B. Charlip. *Handtalk: An ABC of Finger Spelling and Sign Language*. New York: Parent's Magazine Press, 1974.

Conley, Jane Leslie. *Crazy Lady!* New York: HarperCollins, 1993.

Duffy, James. *Uncle Shamus*. New York: Scribner Young Readers, 1992.

Dunn, Kathryn Boessel, and Allison Boessel Dunn. *Trouble with School: A Family Story About Learning Disabilities*. Rockville, Md.: Woodbine House, 1993.

Fassler, Joan. *My Grandpa Died Today*. New York: Human Sciences Press, 1969.

Frim Kline, Dawn M. *Someone Like You*. North Billerica, Mass.: Curriculum Associates, 1989.

Gehret, Jeanne. *Eagle Eyes: A Child's Guide to Paying Attention* (2nd ed.). Fairport, N.Y.: Verbal Images Press, 1991.

Gibson, W. *The Miracle Worker*. New York: Bantam, 1956. (Also good for adults.)

Glover, Nancy. *Speedway Sam: A Book About Spinal Cord Injury for Children*. Birmingham: University of Alabama at Birmingham, 1990.

Gold, P. *Please Don't Say Hello*. New York: Human Sciences Press, 1975.

Gordon, M. *I Would If I Could: A Teenager's Guide to ADHD/Hyperactivity*. DeWitt, N.Y.: GSI Publications, 1993.

Gordon, M. *My Brother's a World Class Pain: A Sibling's Guide to ADHD/Hyperactivity*. DeWitt, N.Y.: GSI Publications, 1992.

Gould, Marilyn. *The Twelfth of June*. Newport Beach, Calif.: Allied Crafts, 1993.

Greenfield, Eloise. *Darlene*. New York: Methuen, 1980.

Greenfield, E., and A. Revis. *Alesia*. New York: Philomel Books, 1981.

Greenwald, Sheila. *Will the Real Gertrude Hollings Please Stand Up?* Boston: Little, Brown, 1983.

Guccione, Leslie D. *Tell Me How the Wind Sounds*. New York: Scholastic, 1989.

Head, Barry, and Jim Sequin. *Who Am I?* Pittsburgh, Pa.: Family Communications, 1975.

Hlibok, Bruce. *Silent Dancer*. Englewood Cliffs, N.J.: Julian Messner, 1981.

Holcomb, Nat. *Sarah's Surprise*. Exton, Pa.: Jason and Nordic Publishers, 1990.

Hunt, Nigel. *The World of Nigel Hunt*. New York: Garrett, 1967.

Johnston, Julie. *Hero of Lesser Causes*. Boston: Joy Street Books, 1992.

Kamien, Janet. *What If You Couldn't......?* New York: Charles Scribner's Sons, 1979.

Killilea, M. *Karen*. New York: Dell, 1983.

Kriegsman, Kay H., et al. *Taking Charge: Teenagers Talk About Life and Physical Disabilities*. Rockville, Md.: Woodbine House, 1992.

Krisher, Trudy. *Kathy's Hats: A Story of Hope*. Morton Grove, Ill.: Albert Whitman, 1990.

Lasker, Joe. *He's My Brother*. Chicago: Albert Whitman, 1974.

Levine, Mel. *Keeping a Head in School: A Student's Book About Learning Abilities and Learning Disorders*. Cambridge, Mass.: Educators Publishing Service, 1990.

Litchfield, Ada B. *A Cane in Her Hand*. Chicago: Albert Whitman, 1984.

Litchfield, Ada B. *Words in Our Hands*. Chicago: Albert Whitman, 1980.

Metzger, Lois. *Barry's Sister*. New York: Puffin, 1993.

Meyers, R. *Like Normal People*. New York: McGraw-Hill, 1978.

Nadeau, K. G., E. B. Dixon, and S. Biggs. *School Strategies for ADD Teens*. Annandale, Va.: Chesapeake Psychological Publications, 1993.

Nolan, Christopher. *Under the Eye of the Clock*. New York: St. Martin's Press, 1987. (Also good for adults.)

Peckinpah, Sam L. *Chester...the Imperfect All-Star*. Woodland Hills, Calif.: Scholars Press, 1993.

Perske, Robert. *Circles of Friends*. Nashville, Tenn.: Abingdon Press, 1988.

Perske, Robert. *New Life in the Neighborhood*. Nashville, Tenn.: Abingdon Press, 1980.

Peterson, Jeanne Whitehouse. *I Have a Sister: My Sister Is Deaf*. New York: Harper and Row, 1977.

Pirner, Connie W. *Even Little Kids Get Diabetes*. Morton Grove, Ill.: Albert Whitman, 1991.

Quinn, Patricia, and Judith Stern. *Putting on the Brakes: Young People's Guide to Understanding Attention Deficit Hyperactivity Disorder (ADHD)*. New York: Magination Press, 1991. (For teenagers.)

Quinn, Patricia. *Putting on the Brakes: A Child's Guide to Understanding and Gaining Control over Attention Deficit Hyperactivity Disorder (ADHD)*. New York: Magination Press, 1991. (For younger girls.)

Radin, Ruth Yaffe. *Carver*. New York: Macmillan, 1990.

Riskind, Mary. *Apple Is My Sign*. Boston: Houghton Mifflin, 1981.

Russo, Marisabina. *Alex Is My Friend*. New York: Greenwillow Books, 1992.

Schweier, Karin M. *Keith Edward's Different Day: Different Is Just Different!* San Luis Obispo, Calif.: Impact Publishers, 1992.

Scott, Sharon. *Not Better...Not Worse...Just Different*. Amherst, Mass.: Human Resource Development Press, 1992.

Shapiro, Lawrence E., and T. Parotte (ill.). *Sometimes I Drive My Mom Crazy, But I Know She's Crazy About Me: A Self-Esteem Book for Overactive and Impulsive Children*. King of Prussia, Pa.: Center for Applied Psychology, 1993.

Shyer, Marlene Fanta. *Welcome Home Jellybean*. New York: Charles Scribner's Sons, 1978.

Sign Language Fun. New York: Random House/Children's Television Workshop, 1980.

Slepian, Jan. *Risk n' Roses*. New York: Philomel Books, 1990.

St. George, Judith. *Dear Dr. Bell—Your Friend, Helen Keller*. New York: Putnam, 1992.

Sullivan, Mary Beth, and Linda Bourke. *A Show of Hands*. New York: J. B. Lippincott, 1980.

Sullivan, Tom. *If You Could See What I Hear*. New York: Harper and Row, 1975.

Swarthout, Glendon, and Kathryn Swarthout. *Whales to See, The*. New York: Doubleday, 1975.

Thompson, Mary. *My Brother Matthew*. Rockville, Md.: Woodbine House, 1992.

Walker, Lou Ann. *Amy: The Story of a Deaf Child*. New York: E. P. Dutton, 1985.

Whelan, Gloria, and Leslie Bowman (ill.). *Hannah*. New York: Knopf, 1991.

Wood, June Rae. *The Man Who Loved Clowns*. New York: Putnam, 1992.

Wright, Betty R. *My Sister Is Different*. Milwaukee, Wis.: Raintree, 1981.

Zeier, Joan T. *Stick Boy*. New York: Atheneum, Maxwell MacMillan International, 1993.

BOOKS FOR ADULTS

Accommodation and Accessibility: Implementing the ADA on a Local Level. New York: American Foundation for the Blind, 1992.

ADA Compliance Guidebook: A Checklist for Your Building. Washington, D.C.: Building Owners and Managers Association International, 1991.

Americans with Disabilities Act Handbook. Washington, D.C.: Equal Employment Opportunities Commission and the U.S. Department of Justice, 1991.

Bornstein, Harry, Karen L. Saulnier, and Lillian B. Hamilton, eds. *The Comprehensive Signed English Dictionary*. Washington, D.C.: Gallaudet University Press, 1983.

Checklist for Existing Facilities: The Americans with Disabilities Act Survey for Readily Achievable Barrier Removal. Albertson, N.Y.: National Institute on Disability and Rehabilitation Research, 1992.

Corlin, Margaret F., et al. *Understanding Abilities, Disabilities, and Capabilities: A Guide to Children's Literature*. Englewood, Colo.: Libraries Unlimited, 1991.

Curran, Eileen P. *Just Enough to Know Better: A Braille Primer*. Boston: National Braille Press, 1988.

Getting, Lindsay, Rosemary Leonard, and Kate O'Loughlin. *Person to Person: Community Awareness of Disability*. Balgowah, Australia: Williams & Wilkins, ADIS Pty Ltd. U.S. distributor/Baltimore, Md.: Paul H. Brookes Publishing, 1986.

Gillespie, John T., and Corinne J. Naden. *Best Books for Children: Preschool Through Grade 6* (5th ed). New York: R. R. Bowker, 1994.

Greenstein, D. *Backyards and Butterflies: Ways to Include Children with Disabilities in Outdoor Activities*. Cambridge, Mass.: Brookline Publications, 1993.

A Guide to Designing Accessible Outdoor Recreation Facilities. Ann Arbor, Mich.: Heritage Conservation and Recreation Service, U.S. Department of the Interior, 1980.

Hammeken, Peggy. *Inclusion: 450 Strategies for Success*. Minnetonka, Minn.: Peytral Publications, 1995.

Including Girls with Disabilities in Youth Programs. Oakland, Calif.: Berkeley Planning Associates, 1996.

Kasser, Susan. *Inclusive Games: Movement Fun for Everyone!* Champaign, Ill.: Human Kinetics, 1995.

Kaufman, Sandra Z. *Retarded Isn't Stupid, Mom!* Baltimore, Md.: Paul H. Brookes Publishing, 1988.

Lovett, Herbert. *Learning to Listen: Positive Approaches and People with Difficult Behavior*. Brooks Publishing, 1996. Order from Institute on Disability, University of New Hampshire, 7 Leavitt Lane, Suite 101, Durham, N.H. 03829-3522.

Managing Inclusive Programs: How to Set Up and Run Inclusive Extended Year Programming. Hampton, N.H.: AGH Associates, Box 130, 1994.

Michaelis, Bill, and Dolores Michaelis. *Learning Through Non-Competitive Activities and Play*. Palo Alto, Calif.: Learning Handbooks, 1977.

Moon, M. S. *Making School and Community Recreation Fun for Everyone: Places and Ways to Integrate*. Baltimore, Md.: Paul H. Brookes Publishing, 1994.

Morris, G. S. Don. *How to Change the Games Children Play*. Minneapolis, Minn.: Burgess Publishing Company, 1980.

Nesbit, Jan, ed. *Natural Supports in School, at Work, and in the Community for People with Severe Disabilities*. Baltimore, Md.: Paul H. Brookes Publishing, 1992.

Opening the Environment for Exploration and Enrichment: Activities for the Special Child. Philadelphia, Pa.: Schuylkill Valley Nature Center, n.d.

Orlick, Terry. *Challenge Without Competition*. New York: Pantheon Books, 1978.

Phillips, Elizabeth. *Women and Girls with Disabilities: An Introductory Teaching Packet*. Brooklyn, N.Y.: Organization for Equal Education of the Sexes, 1986.

Powers, Laurie, George Singer, and Jo-Ann Sowers. *On the Road to Autonomy: Promoting Self-Competence in Children and Youth with Disabilities*. Baltimore, Md.: Paul H. Brookes Publishing, 1996.

Riekehof, Lottie L. *The Joy of Signing*. Springfield, Mo.: Gospel Publishing House, 1987.

Rynders, John E., and Stuart J. Schleien. *Together Successfully: Creating Recreational and Educational Programs That Integrate People With and Without Disabilities*. Minneapolis: University of Minnesota, 1991. Available from The Arc, Publications Department, P.O. Box 1047, Arlington, Tex. 76004.

Schleien, S., et al. *Lifelong Leisure Skills and Lifestyles for Persons with Developmental Disabilities*. Baltimore, Md.: Paul H. Brookes Publishing, 1995.

Smith, Sally L. *No Easy Answers: The Learning Disabled Child at Home and at School*. Cambridge, Mass.: Winthrop Publishers, 1979.

Sternlicht, Manny, and Abraham Hurnitz. *Games Children Play*. New York: Van Nostrand Reinhold Company, 1981.

U.S. Department of Education, Office of Special Education and Rehabilitative Services, National Institute of Handicapped Research. *Directory of National Information Sources on Handicapping Conditions and Related Services*. Washington, D.C.: U.S. Government Printing Office, 1986.

GAMES, KITS, VIDEOS, AND MANUALS

Be My Friend (kit). Canadian Council on Children and Youth, 323 Chapel, Ottawa, Ontario KIN 722.

Building Community: A Manual Exploring Issues of Women and Disability. Educational Equity Concepts, 114 East 32nd Street, New York, N.Y. 10016.

Dream Catchers (video, closed-captioning, available on request). Institute on Disability, University Affiliated Program, University of New Hampshire, 7 Leavitt Lane, Suite 101, Durham, N.H. 03829-3522.

Everybody Counts! A Workshop Manual to Increase Awareness of Handicapped People by J. M. Ward et al. (manual and tape). Council for Exceptional Children, 1920 Association Drive, Reston, Va. 22091.

Everybody Has a Song (tape). Song, P.O. Box 22206, Sacramento, Calif. 95682.

Explore. Champaign, Ill. (manual). Management Learning Laboratories, Sagamore Publishing, n.d.

I'm Not Stupid (kits, videos, etc.). Association for Children and Adults with Learning Disabilities, 4156 Library Road, Pittsburgh, Pa. 15234.

The Kids on the Block (books, kits, puppets). 9385-C Gerwig Lane, Columbia, Md. 21046.

Learning to Play, Playing to Learn: Recreation as a Related Service (manual). Center for Recreation and Disability, Studies and Recreation Administration, University of North Carolina at Chapel Hill, CB #8145, 730 Airport Road, Suite 204, Chapel Hill, N.C. 27514-8145.

Mainstreaming for Equity Activity and Resource Kits. Educational Equity Concepts, 114 East 32nd Street, New York, N.Y. 10016.

More Alike Than Different (kit). Robert M. Stockman and Associates, 445 Figueroa St., #2600, Los Angeles, Calif. 90071.

Regular Lives (video and manual). PBS Video, 1320 Braddoch Place, Alexandria, Va. 22314-1698, (800) 344-3337.

SIGN IT! (sign language game and book). Permanent Reflections, 206 Browning Avenue, Toronto, Ontario, Canada M4K 1X2.

Sunrise at Campobello. Warner Films, Trans-World Films, 332 S. Michigan Avenue, Chicago, Ill. 60604.

Understanding Differences (manual). Learning Trees, P.O. Box 4116, Englewood, Calif. 80155.

Voices of Friendship (open-caption video). Institute on Disability, University Affiliated Program, University of New Hampshire, 7 Leavitt Lane, Suite 101, Durham, N.H. 03829-3522.

A Walk in Another Pair of Shoes (kit). CHANHC, P.O. Box 4088, Los Angeles, Calif. 90051.

What If You Couldn't? (kit). Selective Educational Equipment, 3 Bridge Street, Newton, Mass. 02195.

Yes I Can Program (kit for junior high and high school students). Institute on Community Integration, University of Minnesota, 109 Pattee Hall, 150 Pillsbury Drive, S.E., Minneapolis, Minn. 55455.

GIRL SCOUT RESOURCES (BRAILLE, LARGE TYPE, AND AUDIOTAPE)

Books for the Blind, A Not-for-Profit Corporation, 2123 East 38th Street, Brooklyn, N.Y. 11234, (718) 951-9081.

ORGANIZATIONS

American Council of Rural Special Education (ACRES), Department of Special Education, University of Utah, Milton Bennon Hall, Room 221, Salt Lake City, Utah 84112, (801) 581-8442.

American Foundation for the Blind, 11 Penn Plaza, Suite 300, New York, N.Y. 10001, (212) 502-7600 (voice), (212) 502-7662 (TT), (800) 232-5463.

American Heart Association, 7320 Greenville Avenue, Dallas, Tex. 75231.

American Occupational Therapy Association, P.O. Box 31220, 4720 Montgomery Lane, Bethesda, Md. 20824-1220, (301) 652-2682, (800) 377-8555 (TT).

American Physical Therapy Association, 1111 North Fairfax Street, Alexandria, Va. 22314, (703) 684-2782, (800) 999-2782.

American Red Cross, 17th and D Streets, N.W., Washington, D.C. 20006.

American Speech and Hearing Association, 10801 Rockville Pike, Rockville, Md. 20852.

Americans with Disabilities Act (ADA) Disability Rights Education and Defense Fund, ADA Technical Assistance Information Line, (800) 466-4232 (voice, TTY).

The Arc: A National Organization on Mental Retardation, 500 E. Border St., Suite 300, Arlington, Tex. 76010, (817) 261-6003, (817) 277-0553 (TTY), (800) 433-5255.

Arthritis Foundation, 1314 Spring Street, N.W., Atlanta, Ga. 30309.

Association for Children and Adults with Learning Disabilities, 4156 Library Road, Pittsburgh, Pa. 15234.

Autism Society of America, 7910 Woodmont Avenue, Suite 650, Bethesda, Md. 20814, (301) 657-0881, (800) 3-AUTISM.

Brain Injury Association, 1776 Massachusetts Avenue, N.W., Suite 100, Washington, D.C. 20036, (202) 296-6443.

Centers for Disease Control National AIDS Clearinghouse, (800) 458-5231 (voice), (800) 243-7012 (TTY).

Children and Adults with Attention Deficit Disorders (C.H.A.D.D.), 499 N.W. 70th Avenue, Suite 109, Plantation, Fla. 33317, (305) 587-3700, (800) 233-4050 (voice mail information).

Clearinghouse on Disability Information, Office of Special Education and Rehabilitative Services, Room 3132, Switzer Building, 330 C Street, S.W., Washington, D.C. 20202-2524, (202) 205-8241 (voice, TDD).

Council for Exceptional Children, 1920 Association Drive, Reston, Va. 22091.

Educational Equity Concepts, 114 East 32nd Street, New York, N.Y. 10016.

Epilepsy Foundation of America, 4351 Garden City Drive, Landover, Md. 20785.

Family Resource Center on Disabilities, 20 East Jackson Boulevard, Room 900, Chicago, Ill. 60604, (312) 939-3513, (312) 939-3519 (TT), (800) 952-4199.

Joseph P. Kennedy, Jr., Foundation, 1350 New York Avenue, N.W., Washington, D.C. 20005.

Leukemia Society of America, 733 Third Avenue, New York, N.Y. 10017.

Muscular Dystrophy Association of America, 3300 East Sunrise Drive, Tucson, Ariz. 85718, (602) 529-2000.

National Amputation Foundation, 1245 150th Street, Whitestone, N.Y. 11357.

National Arthritis and Musculoskeletal and Skin Diseases Information Clearinghouse, 1 AMS Circle, Bethesda, Md. 20892-3675, (301) 495-4484.

National Association of the Deaf, 814 Thayer Avenue, Silver Spring, Md. 20910.

National Center for Learning Disabilities, 99 Park Avenue, New York, N.Y. 10016.

National Easter Seal Society, 2023 W. Ogden Avenue, Chicago, Ill. 60612.

National Health Information Center, P.O. Box 1133, Washington, D.C. 20013-1133, (301) 565-4167, (800) 336-4797.

National Information Center for Children and Youth with Disabilities, P.O. Box 1492, Washington, D.C. 20013.

National Information Center on Deafness (NICD), Gallaudet University Press, 800 Florida Avenue, N.E., Washington, D.C. 20002-3695, (202) 651-5051 (voice), (202) 651-5052 (TDD).

National Mental Health Association, 1021 Prince Street, Alexandria, Va. 22314.

National Organization on Disability (NOD), 910 16th Street, N.W., Suite 600, Washington, D.C. 20006.

National Society to Prevent Blindness, 500 East Remington Road, Schaumburg, Ill. 60173.

People First International, P.O. Box 12642, Salem, Ore. 97309.

Special Recreation, 362 Kaser Avenue, Iowa City, Iowa 52240.

Spina Bifida Association of America, 4590 MacArthur Boulevard, N.W., Suite 250, Washington, D.C. 20007, (202) 944-3285, (800) 621-3141.

TASH (Association for Persons with Severe Handicaps), 29 West Susquehanna Avenue, Suite 210, Baltimore, Md. 21204, (410) 828-8274, (800) 482-TASH.

United Cerebral Palsy Association, 66 East 34th Street, New York, N.Y. 10016.

Very Special Arts, John F. Kennedy Center for the Performing Arts, Education Office, Washington, D.C. 20566.

RECREATION AND OUTDOOR EDUCATION

American Alliance for Health, Physical Education, and Dance (AAHPED), 1900 Association Drive, Reston, Va. 22091.

American Camping Association, Bradford Woods, Martinsville, Ind. 46151.

Mobility International U.S.A., P.O. Box 3551, Eugene, Ore. 97403.

National Handicapped Sports and Recreation Association, 1145 19th Street, N.W., Suite 717, Washington, D.C. 20036.

National Park Service, Division of Special Programs and Populations, U.S. Department of the Interior, 18th and C Streets, N.W., Washington, D.C. 20240.

References

ADA Compliance Guide: Americans with Disabilities (1990). Washington, D.C.: Thompson Publishing Group.

Hallahan, Daniel P., James M. Kauffman, and John W. Lloyd (1996). *Introduction to Learning Disabilities*. Boston: Allyn and Bacon.

Hardman, Michael L., Clifford J. Drew, and M. Winston Egan (1996). *Human Exceptionality: Society, School, and Community* (5th ed.). Boston: Allyn and Bacon.

Haring, Norris G., Linda McCormick, and Thomas G. Haring (1994). *Exceptional Children and Youth* (6th ed.). Columbus, Ohio: Merrill Publishing Company.

Heward, William, and Michael Orlansky (1996). *Exceptional Children* (5th ed.). Englewood Cliffs, N.J.: Merrill Publishing Company.

Kauffman, James (1997). *Characteristics of Emotional and Behavioral Disorders of Children and Youth* (6th ed.). Upper Saddle River, N.J.: Merrill Publishing Company.

Lerner, Janet W. (1993). *Learning Disabilities: Theories, Diagnosis, and Teaching Strategies* (6th ed.). Boston: Houghton Mifflin Company.

Meyen, Edward L., ed. (1996). *Exceptional Children in Today's Schools* (3rd ed.). Denver, Colo.: Love Publishing Company.

Meyen, Edward L., and Thomas M. Skrtic, eds. (1995). *Special Education and Student Disability: An Introduction—Traditional, Emerging, and Alternative Perspectives* (4th ed.). Denver, Colo.: Love Publishing Company.

Meyen, Edward L., Glenn A. Vergason, and Richard J. Whelan. *Strategies for Teaching Exceptional Learners in Inclusive Settings* (1996). Denver, Colo.: Love Publishing Company.

Public Law 93-112, Section 504, Rehabilitation Act of 1973.

Public Law 94-142, Part B. Education of the Handicapped Act of 1975.

Public Law 101-336. Americans with Disabilities Act of 1990.

Public Law 101-446. Individuals with Disabilities Education Act, 1990.

Rothstein, Laura (1992). *Special Education Law* (2nd ed.). White Plains, N.Y.: Longman.

Schleien, Stuart J., M. Tipton Ray, and Frederick Green (1997). *Community Recreation and People with Disabilities: Strategies for Inclusion*. Baltimore, Md.: Paul H. Brookes Publishing.

Shames, George H. (1994). *Human Communication Disorders: An Introduction* (4th ed.). New York: Merrill Publishing Company.

U.S. Department of Education (1996). *Seventeenth Annual Report to Congress on the Implementation of the Individuals with Disabilities Education Act*. Washington, D.C.: U.S. Government Printing Office.

Index

A

Absence seizures, 88
Abstract concepts and ideas, 45, 62, 72
Accessibility standards, 10–11
Acquired amputations, 79
Acquired immune deficiency syndrome (AIDS), 91
Acting out, 63
Activities, adapting, 12–15. *See also* Simulation activities
  for behavior disorders, 57–58
  for communication disorders, 41–42
  for hearing impairments, 65–66
  for learning disabilities, 34–36
  for mental retardation, 48–50
  for physical disabilities, 82–84
  for visual impairments, 75–77
ADD (attention deficit disorder), 52, 89
  simulation activities, 18–19
ADHD (attention deficit hyperactivity disorder), 89
Aggressive behaviors, 55, 58
AIDS, 91
"Alice," 24, 26, 27
Allergies, 85–86
  adaptations for girls with, 86
  characteristics of, 85–86
  irritants, 85
American Association of Mental Retardation (AAMR), 43–44
American Juvenile Arthritis Foundation, 80
American Sign Language (ASL), 62–63
Americans with Disabilities Act (ADA), 3, 4
Amputations, 79
Anger, 28, 29, 54, 59, 79, 80
Arthritis, 79–80
Arthritis Foundation, 80
Articulation errors, 39
Artificial limbs, 79
Asthma, 90–91
Atonic/akinetic seizures, 88
Attention deficit disorder (ADD), 52, 89
  simulation activities, 18–19
Attention deficit hyperactivity disorder (ADHD), 89
Attention-seeking behaviors, 31, 54, 55, 59, 63
Attention span, 37, 46, 62, 63
Audiotape books, 73
Autism, 5

B

"Baby talk," 40
Background information, preparing yourself with, 7–8
Background noise, 67
Balance
  loss of, 62
  poor sense of, 31, 79
Bathrooms, analysis of, 11
Behavior disorders, 52–59
  adaptations for girls with, 55–59
  characteristics of, 54–55
  factors in, 52–53
  famous people with, 59
  myths and stereotypes about, 53
  percentage of school-age population with, 5
Behaviors
  aggressive, 55, 58
  appropriate, 3, 36, 53, 59, 80, 91
  attention-seeking, 31, 54, 55, 59, 63
  inappropriate, 36, 48, 54, 55, 58, 59, 63, 85
Bleeding, 80
Blindfold, wearing a, 22
Blindness, 69, 71. *See also* Visual impairments
  percentage of school-age population with, 5
Blinking, 73
Blood sugar level, 86

107

Blurred vision, 69–70
Body image, 70
Boredom, 63
Braille, 10, 11, 69, 74, 77
Braille writer, 73, 74
Brownie Girl Scouts, adapting activities for, 13
Brownie Girl Scout Handbook, 13
Buttoning, difficulty with, 31
Buttoning a shirt, 28

C

Cadette Girl Scouts, adapting activities for, 15
Calculator, talking, 72
Canes, 23, 71
Central hearing loss, 61
Central vision loss, 69
Cerebral palsy, 80–81
Cleft lip or palate, 39
Clothing, 31, 77, 81
Cloudy vision, 69
Color coding, 49
Communication ability, 2–3
   behavior disorders and, 54
   hearing impairments and, 62–63
   mental retardation and, 46–47
   visual impairments and, 72–73
Communication board, 80
Communication (communicating)
   behavior disorders and, 56–57
   hearing impairments and, 65
   learning disabilities and, 32–34
   mental retardation and, 48
   physical disabilities and, 84
   visual impairments and, 74–75
Communication disorders, 38–42
   adaptations for girls with, 40–42
   characteristics of, 39–40
   classification of, 39
   famous people with, 42
   myths and stereotypes about, 39
   percentage of school-age population with, 5
   simulation activities, 28
Comprehension, 40, 46
Computer
   with speech, 73
   talking, 73
Concentration, 45, 54
Conductive hearing loss, 60
Confusion, 32
Congenital amputations, 79
Cotton in your ears, 21
Coughing, 90, 91
Crutches, 23
Crying, 55
Cuts, 14, 80, 81, 88
Cystic fibrosis, 90

D

Dancing activities, 32
Deafness, 61
Definitions of disabilities, 3–4
Developmental delay. *See* Mental retardation
Diabetes, 86–87
Diabetic coma, 86
Diet, 86
Directions, 32
   difficulty following, 46
Disinterestedness, 85
Disruptiveness, 33
Distorted glasses, wearing, 21–22
Distorted vision, 69–70
Distraction, 32, 36, 37, 45, 51, 54, 58
Diversity in Girl Scouting, 2
Dog, guide, 71
Dwarfism, 81
Dysfluency, 39

E

Ears
   draining, 63
   placing cotton in your, 21
   pulling or tugging at, 63
Emotional behaviors, 3
   behavior disorders and, 54–55
   communication disorders and, 40
   hearing impairments and, 63
   learning disabilities and, 33
   mental retardation and, 47
   visual impairments and, 73
Entrances, analysis of, 10
Epilepsy, 87–89, 92
Equilibrium problems, 62
Equipment, for visual impairments, 72–73
Exercise, 79, 81, 85, 86
Eye contact, 7, 54, 57, 80
Eye rubbing, 74

F

Facial expressions, 40, 73, 75
Fatigue, 79, 80, 82, 85–86, 89
Figures of speech, 63
Finger movements, 80
Focus, loss of, 32, 46
Food allergies, 85, 86
Friendships, 33, 47, 55

G

Generalized tonic-clonic seizures, 87–88
Gigantism, 81
Girl Scout Badges and Signs, 13
Grand mal seizures, 87–88
Guide dogs, 71

H

Hallways, analysis of, 10–11
Hard of hearing, 61

Health impairments, 78, 85–93
  famous people with, 93
  myths and stereotypes about, 92
  percentage of school-age population with, 5
Hearing aids, 64, 65–66
Hearing impairments, 60–67
  adaptations for girls with, 64–67
  characteristics of, 62–63
  factors to consider in adapting activities, 60–61
  famous people with, 67
  myths and stereotypes about, 61
  percentage of school-age population with, 5
  simulation activities, 17–18, 21
  speech or language problem with, 39
Hearing loss, 60–61
  severity of, 61
  types of, 60–61
Heart disorders, 89–90
Hesitant behavior, 45
HIV, 91
Hostility, 54
Human immuno-deficiency virus (HIV), 91
Hypoglycemia, 86

I

Identifying cues, 47
Idioms, 63
Immaturity, 36, 46, 47, 62, 85, 89, 90
Immune system, 91, 92
Impulsiveness, 32, 54
Inattentiveness, 37, 62, 63
Inclusion in Girl Scouting, 4–5
Indecisiveness, 47
Individuals with Disabilities Education Act (IDEA), 3, 4
Information, preparing yourself with, 7–8

Insulin shock, 86
Interactions, 40
Interest Projects for Cadette and Senior Girl Scouts, 15
Interruptions, 53, 54, 73
Intonation, 56, 62
IQ (intellectual functioning), 43, 44
Isolation, 40, 54, 58, 63, 67

J

Joking, 47, 62
Junior Girl Scouts, adapting activities for, 13–15
Juvenile rheumatoid arthritis, 79–80

K

Kurzweil reading machine, 73

L

Language impairments, 38–39. *See also* Communication disorders
  percentage of school-age population with, 5
Laziness, 30, 31
Learning ability, 2–3
  behavior disorders and, 54
  hearing impairments and, 62
  learning disabilities and, 32
  mental retardation and, 45–46
  visual impairments and, 72
Learning disabilities, 30–37
  adaptations for girls with, 33–37
  characteristics of, 31–33
  famous people with, 37
  myths and stereotypes about, 31
  percentage of school-age population, 5, 30
  simulation activities, 18–19, 22–23, 24–27

Legal definitions of disabilities, 3–4
Legally blind, 69
Leukemia, 91
"Lion, The," 24, 25, 27
Listening, 73
Listlessness, 79, 85
Location, analysis of, 10
Low vision, 69

M

Mainstreaming, 4
Manual communication, 62–63
Materials, presentation of. *See* Presentation of materials
Math test, 19–20
Medications, 86
Meeting area
  analysis of, 11
  preparing the, 9, 10–11
  visual impairments and, 77
Meetings, 9
Memory
  behavior disorders and, 58
  hearing impairments and, 66
  learning disabilities and, 36
  mental retardation and, 51
  visual impairments and, 77
Mental age, 44, 45
Mental retardation, 43–51
  adaptations for girls who have, 47–51
  characteristics of, 45–47
  definition of, 43–44
  famous people with, 51
  inclusion of girls with, 44
  myths and stereotypes about, 44–45
  percentage of school-age population, 5
  simulation activities, 19–20

109

Mild hearing loss, 61
Mirror writing, 22–23
Mixed hearing loss, 61
Moderate hearing loss, 61
Moodiness, 33, 80, 86
Motor ability, 2–3
    behavior disorders and, 54
    communication disorders and, 40
    hearing impairments and, 62
    learning disabilities and, 31–32
    mental retardation and, 45
    visual impairments and, 70–72
Mouth breathing, 63
Muscles, 45, 81, 88
    tensing, 59, 71
Muscular dystrophy, 91
Myoclonic seizures, 89
Myths and stereotypes
    behavior disorders, 53
    communication disorders, 39
    health impairments, 92
    hearing impairments, 61
    learning disabilities, 31
    mental retardation, 44–45
    physical disabilities, 92
    visual impairments, 70

N

National Library Service for the Blind and Physically Handicapped, 74
Nondisabled girls and
    advantages of including Girl Scouts with disabilities, 5
    helping the girl with a disability, 9
    preparing for arrival of a girl with a disability, 8
    simulation activities for, 16–29
Non-verbal messages, 72

O

Optacon, 73
Oral-aural communication, 63
Oral instructions, difficulty following, 62, 63
Organizational skills
    behavior disorders and, 58
    learning disabilities and, 36
    mental retardation and, 51
Orthopedic impairments. See Physical disabilities

P

Page turners, 83
Paper holders, 85
Partially sighted, 68
Petit mal seizures, 88
Physical ability, 2–3. See also Motor ability
Physical disabilities, 78–85, 93
    adaptations that apply to all, 82–85
    famous people with, 93
    myths and stereotypes about, 92
    percentage of school-age population, 5
    simulation activities, 19, 23, 28, 29
Physical environment, preparing the, 9, 10–11
Posture, poor, 31, 79, 80, 82
Preparing troop, 6–15
    activities, 12–15
    girls, 8
    introducing girl, 9
    the meeting, 9
    yourself, 6–8
Presentation of materials
    behavior disorders and, 57
    communication disorders and, 41
    hearing impairments and, 65–66
    learning disabilities and, 34–35
    mental retardation and, 48–49
    physical disabilities and, 84
    visual impairments and, 75–76
Profound hearing loss, 61
Prosthesis, 79
Public speaking, 28

R

Reading, 24–27, 46, 72, 73, 74
    difficulty, 32, 46
Red eyes, 74
Rehabilitation Act of 1973, 3, 4
Rest periods, 82
Retardation. See Mental retardation
Reward systems, 50
Rocking back and forth, 70

S

Sarcasm, 56
Scapegoating, 47
Section 504 of Rehabilitation Act of 1973, 3, 4
Seizures, 87–89
Self-concept
    creating positive, 59, 82
    poor, 33, 47, 63, 73, 81
Self-confidence, 40, 51, 58
Self-defense, 15
Self-discipline, 31
Senior Girl Scouts, adapting activities for, 15
Sensorineural loss, 61
Sensory abilities, 3
    hearing impairments and, 63
    visual impairments and, 74
Severe hearing loss, 61
Shyness, 63
Sighted guide, 71
Sign language, 62–63, 64, 80

Simulation activities, 16–29
  buttoning a shirt, 28
  placing cotton in your ears, 21
  public speaking, 28
  reading paragraphs, 24–27
  taking a math test, 19–20
  taking a spelling test, 17
  threading a needle, 29
  using mirror writing, 22–23
  using wheelchairs, canes, and crutches, 23
  wearing a blindfold, 22
  wearing distorted glasses, 21–22
  writing and swinging your foot, 18–19
  writing on paper on your forehead, 18
  writing sentences, 18
  writing with pliers, 19
Site analysis, 9, 10–11
Slate and stylus, 73
Social behaviors
  behavior disorders and, 55
  communication disorders and, 40
  hearing impairments and, 63
  learning disabilities and, 33, 36
  mental retardation and, 47
  physical disabilities and, 85
  visual impairments and, 73
Social skills, 44, 47, 60, 81, 89
Speech, 40
  distorted or unusual, 62
  monotone, 62
  quiet or loud, 62
Speech impairments, 38–39. *See also* Communication disorders
  percentage of school-age population with, 5

Spelling test, 17
Spina bifida, 81
Squinting, 73
Stereotypes. *See* Myths and stereotypes
Stubbornness, 63
Stuttering, 39, 41, 42
Supportive behavior
  behavior disorders and, 55–56
  communication disorders and, 40
  hearing impairments and, 64–65
  learning disabilities and, 33–34
  mental retardation and, 47–48
  physical disabilities and, 82
  visual impairments and, 74

T

Telephones, analysis of, 11
Terminal illnesses, 91–92
Threading a needle, 29
Total communication, 63
Totally blind, 69
Traumatic brain disorder, 5
Tunnel vision, 69

U

Unhappiness, 54

V

Verbal outbursts, 54
Vision loss, 68–70
  degree of, 68–69
  kind of, 69–70
  when occurred, 69
Visual impairments, 68–77
  adaptations for girls with, 74–77
  characteristics of, 70–74
  classifications, 68–70
  famous people with, 77
  myths and stereotypes about, 70

percentage of school-age population with, 5
simulation activities, 21–22
Voice disorders, 39

W

Wheelchairs, 10, 11, 81–85, 91
  simulation activities using, 23
Wheezing, 91
White cane, 71
Withdrawal, 58, 63, 85, 91
Work space
  hearing impairments, 66–67
  physical disabilities, 84–85
Writing
  difficulty, 31
  on paper on your forehead, 18
  with pliers, 19
  sentences, 18
  and swinging your foot, 18
  using mirror, 22–23